"Then RUSSELL Said to BIRD ..."

The Greatest Celtics Stories Ever Told

Donald Hubbard

TRIUMPH
BOOKS

To LAW

Library of Congress Cataloging-in-Publication Data

Hubbard, Donald, 1959–
  "Then Russell said to Bird—" : the Greatest celtics stories ever told / Donald Hubbard ; [foreword by] Dave Cowens.
      pages cm
    ISBN 978-1-60078-851-2 (pbk.)
   1. Boston Celtics (Basketball team)—History. 2. Boston Celtics (Basketball team)—Anecdotes. I. Title.
   GV885.52.B67H84 2013
   796.323'640974461—dc23
                              2013020394

This book is available in quantity at special discounts for your group or organization. For further information, contact:
  Triumph Books LLC
  814 North Franklin Street
  Chicago, Illinois 60610
  (312) 337-0747
  Fax (312) 280-5470
  www.triumphbooks.com

Printed in U.S.A.
ISBN: 978-1-60078-851-2
Design by Patricia Frey
Photos courtesy of the New England Sports Museum unless otherwise indicated

Contents

Author's Note

Having had the privilege of previously writing a book about the Boston Celtics, I was doubly thrilled with the opportunity to write another one, this time to relate some of their best stories. Problems arose immediately, because if you are telling a story involving Bill Sharman, it helps to tell the readers, most of whom never saw him play, who he was. And as soon as you do this, you almost have to relate matters chronologically, stories building on other stories, players coming and going.

So I set my course early—a straight vector from the Celtics' first year, 1946, to the present—and then had to eliminate another concern: that many of the finest stories involving this team have already been told. That is where I got lucky; many of them had been long forgotten and just needed to be unearthed.

In doing so, I discovered the pre–Red Auerbach Celtics, the basketball equivalent of the Amazin' Mets, four years of sloppiness and fun. Most Celtics histories skip past those years, relating stories about the first home game, and then the next thing you know, Auerbach is the head coach and begrudgingly accepting "local yokel" Bob Cousy on the team. But the pre-Auerbach Celtics were fun in their own right, and I hope that I have been able to convey that. After the franchise stopped embarrassing itself on the court, it became a joy for another reason, as the Celtics mystique was created and nurtured.

The Celtics mystique differs little from any other sustained winning formula in American sport—stable and committed ownership, excellent management and coaching, and skilled personnel dedicated to the realization of common goals—with one added element. No Celtics team has ever prospered without the leadership of a dominant personality on the court who is nearly manic about winning, whether he be Bill Russell, Dave Cowens, Larry Bird, or Kevin Garnett.

That recurring thread, that essential element, has to be there because of the unique challenges of playing ball in Boston, a town that places incredible pressure on its athletes, rewarding hard work and excellence while decrying half-heartedness. Much like a Notre Dame football program that disproportionately depends on retaining a great coach, given its academic requirements and its gritty rust belt–town home, the Celtics prosper only when that driven player drives his team. It is the elusive ingredient that separates Coca-Cola from sarsaparilla.

Then all of the stories make sense—role players such as Gene Guarilia or Nate Robinson, who perform at levels exceeding their dreams, or men like Bob Brannum or Jim Loscutoff, who punished their bodies to protect Bob Cousy. It explains why guys like Big Ed Sadowski lasted just a year here, back in the days when a player could camp under a basket.

I have watched many Celtics championship games and—before Kevin Garnett and Ray Allen joined Paul Pierce and Rajon Rondo—an awful lot of awful home games on the parquet. Because I still somehow passed on the love of the Celtics to the next generation, it dawned on me that although the titles are great, it's the teams that count. Like a good marriage, the team is there for you in good times and bad, in sickness and in health.

And that's no story.

Introduction

The old basketball thudded, never leaving the nice, rubbery, reverberating sound heard alike on blacktop and state-of-the-art Palestra floors. It resembled a less-rotund medicine ball, not significantly evolved from the original one used by James Naismith in the 1890s to keep young men in fine fettle in the Springfield YMCA. Yet it mattered little how the ball bounced or the cookie crumbled for the Boston Trojans in their one year in the American Basketball League in 1934–35—few fans came out to see them at the Old Boston Arena on St. Botolph Street.

Boston was not a basketball town. Sure, Naismith had founded the sport on the opposite pole of Massachusetts, but a former professional team, the Whirlwinds, had swept out after a brief existence in the 1920s, and the Trojans never caught on. By the spring of 1935 the game disappeared. The City of Boston dropped basketball in its high schools in 1925, as the city's youngsters gravitated toward street hockey and baseball. Their parents devoted themselves to the Bruins in the winter and either the Red Sox or the Braves between thaws.

So when the Trojans played their last game in their last-place, hapless existence, the professional sport ceased to exist in Boston for more than 20 years, unmissed and unlamented, as unpopular as football. Instead, Bostonians rooted for Jimmie Foxx, Lefty Grove, and Ted Williams, or Eddie Shore and Milt Schmidt, as professional basketball kept up its slow and low-scoring pace in the enclaves, barely surviving.

Thud.

But if hoops in Boston had died, Naismith's game flourished elsewhere, particularly with amateurs. More than 10,000 people came out to see talented musician and baller Tony Lavelli of Somerville, Massachusetts, lead his schoolboy team to victory over nearby Waltham. In the college ranks, across the Midwest and most other East Coast cities, crowds gathered to see Adolph Rupp's Kentucky Wildcats or budding Vatican dynasties at St. John's, DePaul, Georgetown, and Notre Dame.

And Holy Cross. Tucked into one of the many steep hills in blue-collar Worcester, Massachusetts, the Jesuits had wisely reinstituted an intercollegiate basketball program in 1939 and, under a dog-faced coach named Doggie Julian, had quietly compiled one of the premier lineups in the country, stocked with players principally from New York City and its burgeoning suburbs. From Xavier High came mountainous George Kaftan, from Chaminade came guard Joe Mullaney, and from Andrew Jackson High came Bob Cousy, a young man who spoke only French until he was five years old, an incredible dribbler whose moves were harder to solve than the Rosetta Stone.

The crusade began as Holy Cross conquered Worcester and its neighboring central Massachusetts mill towns, then stormed the City on the Hill, and soon Boston itself lay prostrate beneath the onslaught. Banned in Boston no more, basketball beckoned, and fans sprang from their triple-deckers and Beacon Hill townhouses, taking trolleys or whisking through the frosty evenings for a night out on the town to see these greats at the Garden.

By 1947, the NCAA fell to the New Yorkers suited up in the purple and white of Holy Cross, as 35,000 people came out in Worcester to welcome their hometown team back for a massive parade. Commented Cousy much later, "I think we lifted basketball in New England, where no one had noticed it before. From that point on, fathers started putting hoops up on garages. High schools started playing basketball. I like to think we were a part of changing basketball in New England."

By then, Walter Brown had opened the Garden doors to the latest incarnation of a professional basketball team in the city, named the Celtics after the legendary barnstormers of the 1920s and early 1930s. Along with some other daring sportsmen and entrepreneurs, he decided to succeed where others fell, to raise America's true national and indigenous pastime to its rightful spot in the pantheon of sport.

The Celtics would fight, and the Celtics would be right, and soon they vanquished everyone.

This time it wasn't a thud—it was an explosion.

chapter 1

The Celtics Begin

The beefy man felt the first fresh air he had experienced in hours, having just done something that might not work or might prove revolutionary, an all-or-nothing type of deal. Having just met with fellow arena owners and a few entrepreneurs, he had joined in on a new venture with them, the formation of a professional basketball league, risky because basketball never seemed to make any money for anyone.

But World War II had just ended, jobs abounded, and people wanted to spend money on entertainment and frivolities again, having submitted to rationing for The Cause. Sucking in the humid July air, Walter Brown jumped on the pavement and began worrying about many things, and surging to the top of the list was, *What the hell did I just do?*

Then he calmed down, as he always did, and began to untangle a myriad of logistics. How to accommodate the new team both for practices and games? Who would help him manage the enterprise? How was he going to get a coach and form a roster, all necessary before opening night in less than four months? Was anyone going to show when the doors opened?

To the manor born was Walter Brown in Hopkinton, Massachusetts, in 1905, a fierce Irish American whose father managed the Boston Garden among other successful entrepreneurial pursuits, and like his contemporaries, the Kennedy boys, he navigated the social reefs inherent in devout Catholic young men making it in an old-money WASP society. No proper Bostonian, he nevertheless attended Phillips Exeter and then helped operate a dingy Boston Garden, warm in the winter, cold in the summer, inhabited by sports lovers and rats alike.

Beloved team founder Walter Brown enjoys a rare moment of relaxation, an anomaly for such an engaged and engaging man.

A big-hearted man, he often popped off and said stupid things, the types of statements that might pitch him into a Sensitivity Training regimen today, but few held it against him because he almost always apologized later. He never grew up and he never grew old, dying before his 60th birthday, venerated at death and honored today by one of Boston University's hockey arenas being named after him, and, for a while, the NBA championship trophy. Most important, a symbolic No. 1 hangs from the latest incarnation of the Boston Garden, because it all started with him and survived only because of his tenacity and belief in a sport he did not particularly enjoy for well over half his life.

He preferred hockey, coaching an American team to its first international gold medal, dismissively referring to basketball as "bounceball." An avid sportsman, he certainly knew about Boston's last failed attempts at founding and cultivating professional basketball clubs and as a businessman appreciated the lunacy of giving Boston a third strike at the sport.

But Walter Brown had seats to fill, having taken over the management of the Boston Garden after his father's untimely death in 1937. Another local institution, Eddie Lee, meticulously kept ledgers of every event planned for the Garden, be it Bruins games, prize fights, circuses, or Communion breakfasts. The Garden had way too many vacant seats, a big old barn sandwiched between the North End and West End of the city.

Besides money and control of the Garden, Brown had another secret weapon perhaps even he did not appreciate: as soldiers and sailors returned from World War II to their homes in Southie and Charlestown, Walk Hill and Jamaica Plain, they got married and had kids, lots of them, named Francis Xavier, Mary Margaret, Mary Katherine, Michael, Thomas, Billy, Caroline, Joseph, and just plain Mary. In the streets off of Blue Hill Avenue, first-generation Bostonian Jews gravitated to basketball, a core group of fans awaiting the professional sport. The Depression had ended, and with a slight hiccup here and there, men had some money to spare to watch their teams play, rather than just read about them in one of the city's still numerous dailies along Newspaper Row.

Some of the best stories surrounding the Celtics are not true; one of the first false gospels asserted that because Walter Brown took so long signing a coach, Honey Russell, the team started off with a disadvantage as their competitors ran off and signed all the best talent first, leaving the Celtics with crummy players. By mid-July 1946, the club had signed Honey—Brown's second choice after Rhode Island State coach Menty Keaney, as Keaney's doctor thought the experience might kill his patient—with Walter Brown establishing his philosophy for assembling his team, stating, "We won't bid fantastic prices against Western industrial teams." Fiscal responsibility ensured that the Celtics, along with the Knicks, emerged as the only original teams in the league to survive to this day in their original cities, yet in the short run consigned Boston to initially unleashing an inferior product on the floor.

Incidentally, at this time Boston had a coach but still no nickname, with renowned sports scribe Harold Kaese endorsing "The first nickname offered [which] was the Boston Yankees, an extremely bright suggestion." Had Brown listened to that sports scribe, fans in the 1940s at Fenway Park who hollered "Yankees suck!" most likely would have referred to their own basketball team and not the opposing baseball club from the Bronx.

Thankfully this did not occur, but still Brown had a team without a name; neither did he have much of a staff, but he did have Howie McHugh, an astute salesman who marketed his product through all the plagues that wiped out almost all of the founding franchises of the new league. He huddled with Brown to christen their creation. Whirlwinds came up at one point, a nod to the long-defunct Boston basketball club, but why saddle the new club with a failed past? The most famous basketball team of all time was the Celtics, a dominant group of barnstormers spawned from the tough west side neighborhoods of New York, such as Hell's Kitchen; one year they ran up a record of 193–11–1. They had whittled away by the 1930s, finally dying, but with Boston having such a teeming Irish population, it seemed natural to dub the club the Celtics, a delusion of grandeur for what initially became a gaggle of misfits with no illusions.

Linking the new club to the original Celtics, it was reported at the time that Honey Russell played for the old New York Barnstormers in 1919, though probably he did not. He apparently once suited up to play football as "Reggie Russell" for George Halas and the Chicago Bears in 1928, later switching back to his status as "one of the greatest guards that ever stepped on a basketball court." After playing thousands of games as a professional, he coached thereafter most notably at Seton Hall, though Brown signed him away from Manhattan College with a three-year contract.

A keen storyteller, Russell recalled playing at the old Boston Arena shortly after the end of World War I, which "had the floor laid over the ice, was cold as a refrigerator, and had the baskets upside down and two feet too high when the gates were opened." Recalled Russell,

"Boston was always good basketball territory, but the pro game didn't click, because it never had adequate halls, didn't have proper publicity and promotion, and lacked players. Now it has everything."

Everything but players, as it transpired. Maybe Menty Keaney's doctor knew what he was talking about.

An old hockey man like Walter Brown, Howie McHugh once guarded the net for Dartmouth but seamlessly shifted much of his devotion to the hardwood to ensure this new venture survived in Boston. A natural at public relations, McHugh saw the game flourish in large part due to his exertions as team publicist, and in time he became the franchise's greatest fan, screaming obscenities at offending referees such as Sid Borgia. Not restricting his communications to refs, he once requested some coins from the Celtics trainer during a tough game in Philly, made worse by some hecklers. Currency in hand, he approached the hecklers and punched them both in the mouth. Once, so excited about the return to action of a Celtic player in the early 1960s, he grabbed the phone to call a sports reporter back in Boston, speaking on the wrong end of the receiver the entire time. The McHugh/Splaver Tribute to Excellence Award, named after Howie and Bullets PR man Marc Splaver, is awarded annually to honor an NBA executive for excellence in the public relations field.

Although he played hockey in college, PR man Howie McHugh helped popularize the Celtics during his tenure. If not for McHugh, fans in Beantown might today be cheering on the Boston Whirlwinds.

chapter 2
A Taste of Honey

In that first NBA season, the Washington Capitols dominated, with their head coach, Red Auerbach, leading his charges to victories in more than 80 percent of the games that they played, although oddly they failed to win the league championship. Boston had Honey Russell, and Washington had piss and vinegar. The Capitols had some stars too, but most teams gravitated toward picking up local collegians; Washington picked off a bunch of Hoyas, Chicago went after Loyola and Notre Dame, and so forth. Except Boston, which ignored Holy Cross and Boston College and instead picked up two players who never attended college, a rarity then.

Lacking in seasoning and experience, Brown also signed Mel Hirsch, the shortest man to ever play in league history before Tyrone Bogues and Earl Boykins laced up more than 40 years later. The club rounded up five men in New York and brought them aboard. Again, Brown shied from stars with large contracts in a venture haunted by the specter of bankruptcy.

So after Honey Russell had signed on, he found a bare cupboard, and of course opposing coaches such as Auerbach exploited these roster weaknesses. Other than assemble the finest professionals in the country and pay them, the Celtics explored every alternative to construct their team. For instance, when NYU baller Johnny Simmons came up to Boston, driven by his "little" brother Connie (who had never played college ball), Honey and his assistants astutely recruited the younger brother on the spot, the best signing they made that year. Johnny played only for a year, but his little 6'8" brother enjoyed a career stretching into the mid-1950s.

Before Chuck Connors wrecked the backboard, another game had already wrapped up in the Arena that evening as the North Cambridge Knights of Columbus defeated the Pere Marquette Knights of Columbus. These warmup games went on for years, generally involving competing fraternal or neighborhood groups, undoubtedly to sell tickets to the friends and family of the players in the first game who wanted to see their favorite son play at the great Arena or Garden. Meanwhile, across town, there was no shortage of potent potables poured into glasses as John F. Kennedy won his first election as a United States Congressman.

Still, Boston did not lack for stars, as it signed Kevin "Chuck" Connors, who later relocated to Hollywood as the lead in the old *Rifleman* television series—quite a feat for a kid from Brooklyn. Thanks to the proliferation of cable channels, reruns of Connors' show have returned, with even fewer basic formats than Auerbach plays. In most episodes, the Rifleman's son gets kidnapped, saved only by the timely intervention of some local nut job or town coot.

Awaiting the day to commence his natural calling, Connors had everyone laughing from the start, sitting in bars, holding court by reciting long poems and stories from heart. One of his more entertaining moments occurred in the very first home game in team history as the Celtics warmed up in the Boston Arena, now Northeastern University's Matthews Arena. Shut out of the Garden by a rodeo show, Connors heaved up a shot, shattering the backboard.

Having no replacement board in the building, Howie McHugh raced across town to the Garden to pick up a new one, only to find some bulls standing between him and his glass backboard. Fortunately, McHugh rousted up some buzzed cowhands to grab the backboard without being mauled, and after he loaded up his prize, sped back to the Boston Arena. Meanwhile, the Celtics, resplendent in their striped socks, shorty shorts, belts, and shirts that looked like cheap softball tees, entertained their fans by engaging in a free throw shooting contest as bored spectators began to exit the building like a fire had broken out. Too bad. They missed a good game as Boston lost to the Stags in overtime 57–55.

Having coached Connors at Seton Hall, Russell knew the Rifleman was lucky to have even hit the backboard that night but kept him on if only to enhance the gate. Recalled Connors years later, "I'm positive my greatest value to the Celtics was as an after-dinner speaker. It seems to me I did more public speaking for the team than playing that first season. They sent me all over New England on speaking engagements. I'd pick up $25 or $50 an appearance, whatever the traffic would bear. When I wasn't apologizing [for the few wins the team had], I was doing things like 'Casey at the Bat' and 'Face on the Bar Room Floor.' I did 'Casey' at the Boston Baseball Writers Dinner that first winter, and Ted Williams was there too, after winning the 1946 American League MVP Award. Ted was very kind to me and laughed his head off at my rendition. Afterward, he said to me, 'Kid, I don't know what kind of basketball player you are, but you ought to give it up and be an actor.' So doing those after-dinner speeches was my raison d'etre."

Having haphazardly assembled a team, Russell watched his men lose 10 of their first 11 games, finally winning a couple against the Pittsburgh Ironmen, a team more woeful than his own. Only the classic upcoming Notre Dame–Army football game and the nearly complete absence of interest generated by the Celtics saved poor Honey Russell.

Other than Connie Simmons, Honey Russell coached only one decent player, small forward Al Brightman. Honey lost Brightman after that first season in peculiar fashion; it seems Brightman and his wife had driven across the country from Seattle to Boston for his second year, but Al had left his wallet home and headed back to Seattle to retrieve it…and never came back East. Eventually, Brightman became a coach himself, cultivating Seattle University into a national powerhouse and in later incarnations coaching in the ABA and operating one of Chuck Connors' resorts.

The roster that year revolved at the expense of evolving. Everyone was technically a rookie, but some ballers had seen their first hardwood floor during WWII; others, like Connie Simmons, had just polished off their high school civics courses. The alliterative Virgil Vaughn from Western Kentucky laced up for 17 games and shot at a .192 clip from the floor, while Don Eliason attempted only one field goal in his NBA career. He missed.

Billeted in rooms in the annex of the Boston Arena, the players had to lie on undersized beds on the occasions they traveled and did not have to catch their sleep on the train. Or buses.

Poor players hampered Coach Russell that first year as his men staggered to a 22–38 record, but the Celtics survived as a franchise, no mean feat as Toronto, Cleveland, Detroit, and Pittsburgh folded. The game bored its fans, with poor shooters, no three-point shots, and no shot clock to prevent teams from freezing the ball with endless passing. At times the game resembled the siege of a castle, with set shots resembling the deliberate firing of medieval catapults.

Presenting the inaugural edition of the Boston Celtics! The 1946–47 squad was coached by Honey Russell (seated, with basketball).

Admitted Honey, the basketball season is "not too long for the players; it's too long for the coaches." After one trying game on the road, Russell addressed his charges by imploring them, "I know you're all nuts, but I have to go home and I'm leaving you on your own. Please act like gentlemen." Instead, they stole "the tail off the buffalo in the railroad station and wound up in [jail]." Imagine Walter Brown's response to that one: "Come again? They stole the what off the what, where?"

Trimmed down to eight teams, the NBA endured for a second autumn, with the Celtics profiting principally from the addition of Ed Sadowski, a pickup in the dispersal draft from the defunct Cleveland Rebels. Fueling the insanity, in their one year of existence the Rebels had dominated the Celtics, winning four of their six contests, yet they ceased operations. By living to fight another year, the Celtics scooped up Sadowski, for free, and made the playoffs, quite undeservingly considering they posted a 20–28 record. In a low-scoring league with only 48 games (a reduction of 20 percent of their contests from the previous seasons), Big Ed scooped rebounds and scored 910 points, earning first-team league-wide honors while alienating everyone on the parquet.

A prince to begin with, Big Ed crowned himself a gold-plated pain in the ass in a December practice at the Arena, as Honey cajoled his star to make more free throws, observing that he had clanged a number of them in a recent game.

Big Ed got defensive, a trait that the plodding gentleman was not known for on the court. "I missed three; the papers said four," he claimed.

Replied Honey, "Well, whatever it was, you missed ones you shouldn't miss, and it's all from lack of practice."

"Ah, you can throw all you want in practice. In a game, either they go in or they don't. I'm not changing my style of shooting."

Russell roared back, "No one asked you to change your style of shooting, but you'll practice shooting every day here. I'm boss here. You're not!"

"You can give me my release right now," concluded Big Ed.

Former *Boston Globe* scribe George Sullivan heard another great story about Big Ed, this one from Howie McHugh:

Sadowski was a pip. Once during a game in Boston, he wasn't getting the ball often enough to suit him, so he called a timeout. "See those people up there?" he asked in the huddle, gesturing toward the stands. "Those people came to see Big Ed score. But Big Ed can't score if Big Ed doesn't shoot the ball. And Big Ed can't shoot the ball if Big Ed doesn't have the ball. So let's pass the goddamn ball to Big Ed!"

Forget what you think or what you have heard about Sidney Wicks, Curtis Rowe, Dino Radja, or Rasheed Wallace—Big Ed was the absolute

Big Ed Sadowski lasted just one year as a Boston Celtic. A defensive-minded, team-first precursor to Bill Russell, he was not.

worst player in Celtics history with respect to embracing a bad attitude or exhibiting an utter devotion to cluelessness. At least he never claimed that there was no "I" in Sadowski.

It did not take a genius to recognize Big Ed failed to grasp the team concept, though if Walter Brown or Honey Russell needed one, they had a future Rhodes Scholar on their roster that year, George Munroe.

Eventually tempers moderated, and Big Ed, who had played for Honey not only with Boston but with Seton Hall, temporarily settled down. But embers of resentment persisted, as the club actively tried to move him for the rest of the season, all the while clogged by their temperamental star's "dour personality, constant bickering with teammates, and utter disdain for the rudiments of defensive play."

Incidentally, those charges were leveled by *Boston Globe* beat writer Jack Barry, who excoriated Sadowski in a column. Big Ed got so riled that he wrote a reply, in the self-appointed asinine guise as "The Condemned Man Speaks," defending himself with his statistics, none of which measured his lack of heart, petulant behavior, or plodding down the court like the snapping turtles he modeled his existence after.

The distractions probably did not lubricate the development of forward Connie Simmons, who shot erratically until the club traded him late in the season to the Bullets for Mike Bloom, a bad trade, as Simmons regained his touch and haunted his old team for several years thereafter, mostly as a Knickerbocker.

But the Celtics made the playoffs, losing to the Stags in a best-of-three series, all played in Boston, as the pivotal pivot man Ed Sadowski led in each game with missed foul shots. So much for ceaselessly practicing free throws. By contrast, the Stags had a gamer, Max Zaslofsky, who carried his team to the next round, as the Honey Russell death watch commenced.

Big Ed drove everyone crazy, but sagely Walter Brown treated his franchise like an army playing in the board game Risk. Survival was key, because wiping your opponents off the floor took precedence over defeating them on the court, and if the Celtics outlived their opponents, they proceeded to scarf up star players in the dispersal draft of the defunct franchises. That's why one does not hear about the heroics of Michael Jordan or Derrick Rose gallantly willing the Chicago Stags to glory.

Honey Russell did not overly impress Celtics owner Walter Brown, but he did make a valuable contact in Boston with Braves owner John Quinn, who hired him as a scout. In that capacity Russell signed Joe Torre, Earl Williams, Don McMahon, and Hank Fischer. He later scouted for the Montreal Expos.

In all fairness, the Celtics did undertake a number of measures unwittingly designed to prematurely end their existence. Emulating the original barnstorming Celtics of yore, they rounded out their original roster with every Irish and Jewish baller from New York, cornering the market on all of the talent necessary for success—in the 1920s. They harked back to the glorious past of another Celtics of a faraway time. Particularly in the first year, they should have recruited BC and Holy Cross grads or men who came from New England and wanted to stay around home, rather than try to swing rent and feed a family on a ballplayer's salary out of state. Attendance at the Boston Arena and Garden stunk; reason dictated that they might want to lure some local legends, so at the very least the player's mom and pop might buy tickets. Also, they should have hired Red Auerbach as their first coach. Conceded Honey, over a decade after his axing, "Walter Brown knew from the start that he needed a Russell, but I was the wrong Russell."

The Celtics needed more work than Joan Rivers.

chapter 3

Dead, Then Red

Having endured two dreadful seasons, the Celtics changed course, deciding to inject their roster and brain trust with the patina of success of
Holy Cross basketball, then a national power. Barely a week after Honey
Russell had coached his last game against the Stags, the Celtics ensconced
themselves in purple, hiring Doggie Julian, a Hall of Famer in the making
(inducted in 1968 almost exclusively for his seasons at Holy Cross), and
as the season progressed, finally inking some Crusader alums.

The Rick Pitino of the McCarthy era, Doggie initially received the
undying love of the Boston fans and media, greeted as a savior, the man
who relentlessly transformed Holy Cross into the finest program in the
nation. One past Crusader game impressed Walter Brown the most.
"With Holy Cross out ahead by about 50 points, nobody got up and
walked out to of the building," he said. "That's the kind of basketball
people want. It is the kind we of the Celtics want to give them."

But first they had to take out the trash.

On May 1, 1948, they traded their best player, Ed Sadowski, to the
Philadelphia Warriors for two centers with nowhere near as much skill,
Chick Halbert and Dutch-born Hank Beenders. Sadowski subsequently
starred for Philly while Beenders suited up for a mere eight games the
next year; the Celtics swapped Halbert in the middle of the ensuing
season. The trade centered around dumping the talented Sadowski,
widely blamed for his team's poor performance because he could not play
nicely with others, particularly his teammates. Even though Boston had
catered to Sadowski, basing its entire offense around him, he had blub-
bered so much that everyone knew he had to go. Sadowski vanished from
Hub Hoopdom forever, though he once coached professional basketball,

earning a 3–9 record, one he undoubtedly deserved. Wonder if he urged his charges to practice their shooting from the charity stripe?

Still, it constitutes to this day one of the worst trades executed by the front office, redeemed by the fact no one remembers it or cares. Until Bill Russell first wore his black shoes on the parquet, the team consistency lacked a presence down low.

The team had rid itself of its reigning jerk, but no stars emerged to replace him. Under their new coach, the Celtics lost 10 straight in January 1949, just missing setting the then-league record for futility. Fortuitously, the timely addition of Holy Cross Crusader stalwarts George Kaftan and Dermie O'Connell stopped the bleeding, as the team began to win here and there, elevated from dreadful to the threshold of mediocrity. The Golden Greek, George Kaftan, ventured east from Holy Cross with Julian but never duplicated his success in the pros, and yet, he was a good player in a group that lacked them. The club struck out in the draft that year, as it generally did back then, though Kaftan at least scored more than 1,500 points in his career, which no other rookie accomplished in the pre-Auerbach drafts. Without Sadowski, the club harmoniously lost, registering an identical win percentage, with or without him.

A first-team All-American at Holy Cross as a sophomore, George Kaftan led the Crusaders to the national championship that year, chosen as the Outstanding Player of the NCAA tournament. He played in the Final Four as a junior and then left midway through his senior season to become a Celtic. A 6'3" center, he never thrived in the pro game, even when shifted to forward.

In the "anything to make a buck at the gate" department, the club staged a night in the season finale for the departing forward Art Spector, the last of the remaining original Boston Celtics. More than 200 young men had suited up at various times during the season or in exhibitions for the green, leaving a bemused Art to reminisce about the past three years, not fully signed on to the idea of retiring. Spector did come back briefly for Boston the next year, at which time an era ended forever.

Spector's lot, and the situation he shared with other league pioneers, aspired to the unglamorous, never reaching even that threshold. Because most of the teams based themselves in the East Coast or Midwest, rail travel was common, and Spector recalled many nights on the train when he simply could not sleep, gazing out a window into the abyss.

In Boston, Doggie Julian used to bark at his men, "You always have to play hard. You have to love the game. If you don't, you'll find yourself out driving a cab somewhere." Years later one of Doggie's former forwards, Johnny Bach, heard a taxi driver honk a horn at him and then saw former Celtics teammate John Ezersky behind the wheel, yelling out, "Tell that SOB Julian that his prediction came true."

Though he had some good players on the team in 1949–50, the team played markedly worse for Julian in his second year at the helm. Julian failed at the professional level, yet he never had the personnel of the Lakers, who in his last year opposing them had four future Hall of Famers on the court: George Mikan, Slater Martin, Vern Mikkelsen, and Jim Pollard (five, if you include Bud Grant, who laced up with Minneapolis for two seasons before shifting over to the NFL, earning enshrinement in Canton in 1994). Julian was overmatched and outgunned.

Ultimately, Doggie Julian squired the team to a .417 winning percentage in 1948–49 and a .324 percentage in 1949–50, far out of the playoffs on each occasion. Julian had no chance, a sad-sack coach saddled with a lack of premier talent, though he did have one player of note in his last season: Somerville native and Yale graduate Tony Lavelli entertained the fans with his virtuoso accordion playing at halftime for $125 a pop. Lavelli's mere presence once helped lure more than 10,000 fans to a high school basketball game when he starred for Somerville, but he did not possess the same élan after he entered pro ball.

Embarrassed by a fourth cruddy season, Walter Brown let the Dog out and nearly terminated the franchise altogether, having sustained massive losses during the past campaign. A minor controversy arose when Julian negotiated with Dartmouth to become its head coach while still serving in Boston, but it passed over quickly, mainly because Brown had already started looking for a better alternative. The Celtics hemorrhaged money as they lost 11 of their final 12 games, mercifully ending their descent with a double-overtime loss to the Knicks on St. Patrick's Day. Said a downtrodden Doggie, in announcing his resignation less than a week later, "I don't think I am tough enough for professional basketball."

Most Celtics fans know that the No. 1 hanging from the Garden rafters with the other retired numbers (and name) honors founder Walter Brown, but perhaps a "1A" banner should be hung for Lou Pieri. Pieri, an old hockey man like Brown, had owned the Providence Steamrollers until their demise in 1949. To this day, Pieri's little Steamrollers who couldn't still hold the NBA record for fewest wins in a season with six (in a 48-game season). Barely hanging on himself, Brown brought Pieri and his infusion of capital to Boston, installing Pieri as minority owner and saving the franchise from financial collapse, thanks also in part to Brown taking out a mortgage on his home and shaking the couch cushions for loose change. After Brown died in 1964, Pieri became half-owner with Walter Brown's widow, and by the next year, they had sold the Celtics to Knickerbocker Beer. Pieri died in 1967.

On April 23, 1950, at the Boston Common, Billy Graham mesmerized 40,000 of the faithful and the anti-Communistic, which back then meant the same thing, in front page news in the following day's editions of the local papers. Couched in Jerry Nason's column in the sports pages of the *Boston Globe*, Celtics owner Walter Brown imparted much more fire and brimstone, threatening to leave the league unless many of his demands were met, including buying out the St. Louis Bombers franchise so that he might pick off their players. For the Boston Celtics, extinction beckoned.

chapter 4

When a Cigar
Is Not Just a Cigar

1950–51

The Celtics began wearing black sneakers.

The Celtics introduced Arnold "Red" Auerbach as their new head coach on April 27, 1950, at a press luncheon in Boston, and this is where the story of the dynastic Celtics begins. Virtually no one knows this, but as Auerbach pointed out at the press conference, his hiring as coach constituted his second stint with the Boston Celtics. In the fall of 1950, Duke University hired him as an assistant coach to help the ailing Gerry Gerald, and during that time, Red served on "payroll" as a Celtics scout, or so he told everybody. Hired as the Tri-Cities Blackhawks coach in mid-November of 1949, he almost broke .500 with a pitiful team and an awful owner named Ben Kerner. Auerbach got fed up with Kerner and left in the spring of 1950, in time for the Celtics to sign him; although his hiring had not formally occurred until the day of the luncheon, he unofficially had been assisting the team leading into the draft a couple of days earlier.

Negotiating with Walter Brown, Auerbach demanded a three-year contract, at which point the Celtics owner opened up the books, marinating in red ink, and persuaded the new coach to take it one year at a time. And that is how Brown and Auerbach operated together from that day forward—one year and a handshake at a time—so legend has it. But after that first year, Walter Brown was quoted as affirming that Red Auerbach had just signed on for a three-year extension. Perhaps he did,

A well-known fact that bears repeating: the Celtics would not be the franchise they are today had it not been for Arnold "Red" Auerbach.

but that misses the larger point: Red had not gotten along with his previous team's owner at all, and his relationship with the at-times hot-headed Brown possessed all of the earmarks of a train wreck, but they worked well together. They were two *mensches* who wanted to win; they trusted each other and produced a successful result. Financially the Celtics still saw little green for a while, but the franchise now rested on solid footing with its management.

Having threatened to pull the Celtics out of the NBA, Brown saw the league attempt to pacify him by buying out the St. Louis and Anderson clubs and distributing their players in a dispersal draft while three other teams ceased existing in the NBA, the original Denver Nuggets and the Sheboygan, Wisconsin, and Waterloo, Iowa, clubs. Brown again got what he wanted simply by surviving, obtaining future Hall of Fame center Easy Ed Macauley in the dispersal draft, after the extinction of his old club, the St. Louis Bombers.

Previously, with the first overall choice, Boston had drafted "lanky" center Chuck Share from Bowling Green, passing up the opportunity of snatching Holy Cross star guard Bob Cousy, the third player taken overall, by Tri-Cities (Cooz is sometimes listed fourth, as the Warriors chose Bob Arizin with a territorial pick). Here was the hoped-for pivot man that the team lacked since Big Ed Sadowski shot himself out of town.

Many local fans expressed disappointment over losing out on Cousy, a man "who seemed such a natural fit for Boston," but the greatest controversy erupted over the drafting of forward Chuck Cooper, the NBA's first African American player. Cooper had previously intimated to Doggie Julian and Celtics forward Art Spector that he wanted to play in the NBA, so the club knew that if it chose Cooper, it would not waste a draft pick. As the *Boston Globe* reported Walter Brown saying at the time, "I hope [Cooper will] be with us a long time."

Local haters and morons did not protest much, but Harlem Globetrotters founder Abe Saperstein melted down over Boston [and Washington's] recent selection of African American players, feeling that this encroached on his self-appointed role of monopolizing black talent. Saperstein threatened to boycott Boston and D.C., causing Walter Brown to explode, "[Saperstein] is out of the Boston Garden now, as far as I'm concerned." See you in hell, Mr. Saperstein.

Having made it apparent that he wanted no part of the flashy Bob Cousy, Red ended up with the Cooz washing back to his shores. Tri-Cities could not afford him so they sold him to the Chicago Stags, who

Perhaps the Celtics have not retired the number of their first African American athlete, Chuck Cooper, because they are uncertain as to what his number was: the 11 on his jersey or the 20 on his shorts.

promptly went bust. His rights then went into the dispersal draft, which had become almost an annual event in professional basketball at that time. Walter Brown let two other clubs choose players before him, a valiant gesture if indeed the commissioner placed number values to the players, making it apparent whom they were choosing when names were placed in a hat. If so, the two other franchises knowingly passed on Bob Cousy and as of October 5, 1950, with the new season commencing in less than a month, Auerbach and the Cooz were stuck with each other.

chapter 5
Cooz

Bob Cousy grew up in New York, with his last address in Yorkville, then a largely German area of the city, now a tony enclave. The neighborhood was very rough in Cooz's era, recalling a time when "the games were stickball and breaking windows." An old *Sports Illustrated* article makes it sound as if his high school coach was as poor a talent evaluator as Michael Jordan's coach later proved, as Cousy did not make the basketball team until his junior year.

Many of his contemporaries, immigrants' kids from mean streets throughout the country, moved out of the big cities altogether, products of postwar affluence or white flight. Sure, they attended weekly Mass at Our Lady of the Declining Ethnic Neighborhood, but they possessed street smarts and swagger before anyone knew what that meant. Cousy's way out led him to Holy Cross College in Worcester, a program that just reinstituted basketball in 1939 but under head coach Doggie Julian had cultivated talent and transformed the Crusaders into one of the premier intercollegiate programs. Doggie's approach to recruiting ventured into the weird; he sent the prized recruit a letter essentially saying, "I hear you're a hot shot. Let's see what you got."

Doggie looked like a dog, but his players were indomitable, as they won the 1946–47 NCAA championship during Cousy's freshman year, led by other stars such as George Kaftan and Joe Mullaney. Cousy repeatedly won some level of All-America honors each of his remaining years of eligibility, but Auerbach remained impassive to New England fans' missives and vocal pleas to pick the Holy Cross star with the first pick. To them, Auerbach defiantly growled, "I don't give a damn for sentiment or names.… That goes for Cousy or anybody else. A local yokel doesn't bring more than a dozen extra fans into your building."

Rubbing it in, Red positively turned scarlet in his "I don't give a damn" speech by stating, "I don't regard Cousy as good as Leede." Confused about what he was saying, as you've never heard of anyone named Leede? Edward Horst Leede was a Dartmouth grad who had just completed his rookie season in Boston and would enjoy just one more year with the team and in the league. Ed Leede was a talented ballplayer but never the equal of Cooz, a man who outscored him by more than 16,000 points in his career.

An improvisational genius, Cousy shredded the competition as soon as Red let him handle the ball, and since Worcester and Boston's metrowest burghers had long since adopted the guard as their own, the club had a draw with a built-in fan base. Soon thereafter, Auerbach crumbled, once admitting that even at practices, "All the other players just want to stand still and watch him." Often no one saw him, as even on his off days, Cooz practiced alone in an otherwise vacant Worcester gym.

Folklore has it that Auerbach, after he took over in Boston, acted like Allen Klein did later with the Beatles and Apple Records and just started firing people and causing secretaries to duck into offices, swallowing gobs of aspirin. Not true. Auerbach, of course, saved the Celtics, but some players had already decided to leave professional basketball before Red was hired, Howie Shannon among them.

The first non-territorial pick in the college draft after the 1948 season—chosen over all-world Alex Groza and other stars such as future Hall of Famer Dick McGuire—Shannon played well for the Providence Steamrollers his rookie season, finishing in the top 10 league-wide in field goal percentage and top five in free throw percentage, as he achieved Rookie of the Year status in the BAA. After the Steamrollers disbanded after his first year, Boston obtained Shannon in the dispersal draft, where he finished both third in team scoring and assists for his new team. Then he disappeared from professional basketball, immediately accepting the coaching position at Topeka High School, eventually serving a successful seven-year stint as the head coach of the Virginia Tech Hokies. So Red never had him to dump.

Amid all of the controversy on draft day, Chuck Share never played for the Celtics, a club that dearly needed a rebounder at the pivot, opting to play for Waterloo, which had jumped to the rival NBL. Walter Brown refused to outbid the Iowa club, which reportedly gave Share a bonus and a five-figure contract, but the Celtics retained his rights—the NBA saw to that. Brown stated that he did not want to pay the rookie more than Ed Macauley, though he did eventually sign Bob Cousy for $9,500. Of course, it did save Red the potential headache of Chuck and Sonny Hertzberg following the musical footsteps of Tony Lavelli in forming a group named, you guessed it, Sonny and Share.

The Boston Red Sox once had a relief pitcher named Sammy Stewart who laconically claimed that spring training games did not "mean dog," but with the Celtics under Auerbach, at least in that first year, they did, as the Celtics began to mow down their opponents. In the first four years, Boston had wallowed; under Red, they fought, winning most if not all of their exhibitions, the majority of which occurred in such bucolic outposts of Celtic Nation as Houlton, Maine; Burlington, Vermont; and Newport, New Hampshire, with scant reporting of these contests by the Boston dailies.

Training camps usually started with two or three days of drills, running constantly, as Red espoused having the best-conditioned athletes in the league. Thereafter, they scrimmaged and then played other league teams and many local teams to keep the players sharp and market the team around New England. Some of the Celtics' bloodiest encounters came against real local yokels who wanted to show the pros up or beat them up.

chapter 6
My Kingdom for a Pivot

The Celtics' regular season inaugural under Red Auerbach started on a bit of a discordant note, as not only did the Fort Wayne Pistons wax Boston 107–84, but Tony Lavelli announced his retirement from basketball to concentrate on music. It surprised few, as he had held out for more money, a risky proposition for a player suiting up for a franchise haunted by the specter of bankruptcy. As the preseason slate of games whittled down, Lavelli played little and scored less, twisting slowly from the drafty Garden and Arena rafters, like forgotten clothes left out to dry.

Reportedly, Red did not like Lavelli's game or his accordion playing, at one point stating, "He's not tough enough to play pro ball, and I've got no time for sentiment," an emotion seconded by Doggie Julian: "Lavelli, who is a great kid, is not yet ready to play the pivot or do things a full-fledged pro is supposed to do." Lavelli could score when undefended, but increasingly opponents pushed him around, unhinging his game. In any event the professional career of one of the greatest schoolboy basketball players in Massachusetts, and a popular and beloved figure, had stalled. Putting a lie to the whole musical concentration nonsense, Lavelli signed a few weeks later with the Knicks, who dumped him after 30 games.

Very few of the Doggie Julian Celtics played for Red Auerbach. Long John Mahnken served a need, clearing out bodies Ed Macauley had trouble posting up against, while Sonny Hertzberg put up points. Brady Walker could score, and Ed Leede served as a valuable swingman off a good rookie year. Otherwise, everyone else walked the plank.

Long John Mahnken, a man whose name you probably have never heard before, played a large role in delivering Red Auerbach to the Hub. Here's how it happened: Mahnken, a center out of Georgetown, played under Auerbach at Tri-Cities, and Ben Kerner traded Long John to the Celtics without informing Red or obtaining his approval. After that trade, Auerbach decided to quit coaching for Kerner, making Red available when Walter Brown needed a new coach. Mahnken played for three years in Boston with Auerbach and then seemingly disappeared. Toward the end of his life Mahnken resided in a nursing home in Cambridge, Massachusetts, and when an administrator contacted Auerbach for some souvenir for Mahnken, Red got right back to her and sent a photo of the 1950–51 Celtics.

In fact, the Celtics opened their season with three losses before ripping up a seven-game winning streak. Unlike previous additions, this club had winners. Macauley led the scoring, Chuck Cooper helped enormously with rebounds, and Bob Cousy did everything well—scoring, dribbling, passing, racking up assists, and even ending up third in the team in rebounds, not bad for a scrawny and flashy guard.

Days after letting Lavelli resign, Red obtained Harry Boykoff from the Bullets, a big, physical player and a top-five field goal percentage shooter the previous year, and less than a week before Christmas, the team obtained center/forward Bob Harris from Fort Wayne, adding another physical presence up front to complement the talented but skinny Macauley. The highest-paid player in the league at $15,000 per, Boykoff gave lie to the Celtics' cost-saving measures. Not an aficionado of accordion-playing small men, Red increasingly stamped the team in his own pugnacious image, even if he had to pay them. Boykoff, for instance, had grown up in much tougher areas of New York City, the Lower East Side and later Brownsville, once joking that he did not have a middle name because his parents could not afford one.

Ask well-versed trivia fans the identities of all the Celtics' retired names, numbers, and mikes, and he or she invariably can do so by rote; yet few fans ever saw Ed Macauley play or know much about his game. We do know how he obtained his nickname, as he explained, "It was the first time I was appointed captain. We dressed in the basement of West Pine Gym, and it was my role to lead the team from the basement locker room through the door. But nobody followed me when I ran down the court and made a layup. Then I heard people shout, 'Take it easy, Ed.' I didn't realize it, but they were playing the national anthem. That 'Easy Ed' nickname helped me get a lot of attention."

Supposedly Harry Boykoff's shot-blocking prowess led to a rule change, whereby a defender no longer could block a shot on its downward arc. Like Ed Macauley, he would have been disqualified for military service due to his height, but he stood on either side of the height/weight scale rather than standing on it, thereby losing a few inches, entitling him to serve in World War II. The opposite of Ed Sadowski in temperament, there probably is a story why he did not work out in Boston, as the club traded him three months after it picked him off waivers. Perhaps a balky knee abruptly ended his career; in every Celtics photograph of him, even the publicity stills, he has a pad over his right knee. A knee injury had halted his freshman season abruptly at St. John's, years earlier. Regardless, you might have never seen him play but may have seen him later in his life in his role as an actor, appearing in an episode of *Frasier* and a number of commercials.

After the Celtics retired his number, Easy Ed faded from view, having permanently returned to his home years earlier. Bostonians born long after Bob Cousy retired have seen tons of tape on the Garden scoreboard or on television commercials, but there is little available tape that highlights Macauley. Based on win shares at Basketball-Reference.com, Easy Ed keeps great company, with modern big men such as Patrick Ewing and Shaquille O'Neal, but he possessed nowhere near the strength of these types of players and consequently ended up only once in the top 10 in league rebounds and a modest league at that.

Do not expect to hear this anywhere else, but Easy Ed more closely resembles Kevin Garnett after coming to Boston, a thin man who scored, yet even that comparison falls short of the mark. Before he became a

Celtic, Garnett had led the NBA for five straight years in defensive rebounds (twice during that span leading the league in total rebounds). Garnett, had he played against Macauley in the 1950s, would have embarrassed Easy Ed in the low post, but he had that effect on most opponents. Don't dismiss Macauley though; he participated in seven All-Star Games in his 10-year career and earned induction into the Basketball Hall of Fame as soon as he retired, the first former Boston Celtic so honored. His presence on the team instantly made Red Auerbach a smarter coach than Doggie Julian.

Two nights after losing to the Celtics, the Washington Capitols folded in the middle of their season in early January 1951, with Boston selecting its player/coach Bones McKinney in the hastily arranged dispersal draft. McKinney had starred for the Capitols under Red Auerbach in the first two years of the NBA, then known as the BAA, and though he was pretty much washed up as a player when Red brought him to Boston, he stayed in touch with Red and continued to exert a positive influence over the development of the Celtics franchise for years after he played his final game with them.

Boldly, Boston began winning, as Auerbach and his exciting new players had changed the culture of malaise surrounding the club. Hoping that an All-Star Game might lure more fans, particularly in light of the recent college point-shaving scandals emerging, the NBA instituted this classic with Boston hosting the inaugural game on March 2, 1951. Walter Brown pushed for it, secretly hoping for at least 10,000 patrons at the event because the gate at most Celtics games still stunk; he nearly seated 11,000 souls at the eventual tip-off.

No slam dunk or three-point shooting contests warmed up the crowd; most players ate and had some beers at the nearby Union Oyster House and then walked over to the Garden to suit up for the game with their star-saturated uniforms. As customary at the time, men dressed in suits and ties and women wore dresses, a formal event demanding the proper decorum.

The East won handily, led by All-Star MVP Ed Macauley and team-mate Bob Cousy. Macauley did not receive his award that evening; it came retroactively two years later, and more than a half-century after the event, the NBA finally sprang for a trophy for a somewhat bemused Easy Ed.

Hosting the All-Star Game was fun, but returning playoff basketball to Boston provided more tangible evidence that the city deserved the sport. Although the Celtics had finished ahead of their first-round opponent, the Knicks, in the Eastern Division, New York possessed four big bodies: Vince Boryla, Harry Gallatin, Sweetwater Clifton, and former Celt Connie Simmons. Their guards weren't bad either—Max Zaslofsky and Hall of Famer Dick McGuire—yet in what subsequently became a sad refrain in the first half-dozen Auerbach years, the lack of big men in the paint killed Boston.

In the first game of the playoffs against the Knicks, the Celts shot a gruesome 24-of-86, as they bowed at the real Garden. Auerbach installed the first curfew of the year, but it did little good at Madison Square Garden as Boston lost again, quickly knocked out of the playoffs. Clif Keane of the *Boston Globe* excoriated the team, screaming that except for Bones McKinney and Ed Macauley, "the rest of the Celtics basketball team was disspirited (sic), sloppy, and made to look like chumps by the Knickerbockers. [Cousy] the ex–Holy Cross whiz was anything but the phenom he had been through most of the season."

Lost in the criticism was one basic fact: Boston had finally begun to care about basketball.

chapter 7

The First Big Three

1951–52

The year after Boston drafted Chuck Share, it traded him to Fort Wayne for the rights to Bill Sharman, another hotshot guard, this one from California and not an East Coast city. Out west, Sharman personified the traits of the fictional Frank Merriwell, an all-American boy with superb physical talent and stamina, lettering in five high school sports—football, basketball, tennis, track, and baseball. On one typical day, Sharman played a tennis match, then competed in a track meet, winning the javelin and shot put events while placing in the hurdles, and then rounded out the day by starting in a baseball game. Bob Cousy once admitted, "Bill was perhaps the best athlete I've ever been associated with." And it never ceased—at 54 years of age, he defeated Magic Johnson in a foul shooting challenge.

Not only did he participate in all of these sports, but he excelled and probably could have become a championship professional tennis player (he won the Central California tennis tournament right after graduation) and did briefly play major league baseball. After serving in the navy in World War II, he earned plaudits as an All-American basketball player at USC, then signed up with the Brooklyn Dodgers, and briefly joined the major league club for a cup of coffee without ever playing, as he sat and watched his team blow a huge lead to the Giants in 1951. At least he got himself kicked out of a game, even if he never played in one, having irritated an umpire who tossed him out for heckling. Secretly, he probably agreed with the ejection, having admitted at one point that he was high strung.

Still, Sharman kept heeding the siren song of baseball regardless of how much success he enjoyed on the hardwood, admitting that "Basketball was something that interested me, but deep down I was convinced that baseball was going to be the sport where I would succeed." Having excelled at nearly everything he ever tried, he stubbornly pursued the one sport that failed to reward him. His devotion took him to Elmira, St. Paul, Mobile, Pueblo, and Fort Worth, and although he failed to hit under .286 only once, he never hit over .300. Simultaneously, the Boys of Summer stars had largely monopolized Brooklyn's roster by the early 1950s, and although Sharman had little competition at the minor league level, he never broke through again, finally leaving the sport after 1955.

Bill Sharman should have listened to Cardinals Hall of Famer Red Schoendienst, who, after seeing the Celtics play basketball in December 1954, thought Bob Cousy had a future on the diamond, gushing, "What a ballplayer he'd make." Red said not a word about Cousy's teammate Sharman, also on the court that day.

Sharman's stubbornness sprang from a hatred of losing—or at least getting beat. In one of the last games of Sharman's career, Jerry West embarrassed the much older Celtic on the floor, so much so that Sharman finally tried to deck the upstart Laker. Remembering the incident several decades later, West concluded, "Bill was tough. I'll tell you this: you did not drive by him. He got into more fights than Mike Tyson. You respected him as a player." Off the court, he was the greatest of gentlemen.

Interestingly, baseball had brought Sharman to Boston. After having played his first NBA season under Bones McKinney in Washington, D.C., the Pistons picked him up in the dispersal draft after the Capitols folded. Apparently the Pistons front office figured that Sharman meant to dedicate himself to baseball, not basketball, so Detroit swapped him to the Celtics for Chuck Share. It would not be the last time that Red Auerbach not only outsmarted the NBA but MLB as well.

Long before he guided the hated Los Angeles Lakers to 33 straight victories as a coach, Bill Sharman was an eight-time All-Star and four-time champion with the Celtics.

(Quick note on Sharman: he remains 12th all time in the NBA for free throw percentage but does not even squeeze into the top 250 all time for field goal percentage, despite having fallen within the top 10 for six seasons in field goal percentage. The crummy equipment and physical plants of that era caused it to be a very rough time for shooting from the floor.)

Improved techniques, training, nutrition, and other factors explain some of the progress made in the game since the 1950s, but Honey Russell explained the differences in shooting accuracy more concretely, opining, "The ball we used was so big we had to shoot and pass with both hands. And sometimes it was lopsided. They have better equipment now [1971]. They practice more. We had one ball for the whole team to practice with; now they have a ball for every man." So in relative terms for his era, Sharman outclassed most other players from the floor and from the foul line; his achievements shine more because he hit his free throws with bad backboards and big balls.

Boston drafted Ernie Barrett in the off-season, a swingman from Kansas State who played in Boston for a couple years, but a more intriguing draftee, a man who never suited up in the NBA, was an All-American guard from Western Kentucky named Rip Gish. How a man named Rip Gish failed to make a roster of a professional team in the 1950s defies logic, unless of course he went straight to Hollywood, which he did not. Perhaps the name of Gish's college coach, Ed Diddle, negated the advantage of possessing a "can't-miss" sports name.

Now the Celtics had an All-Star center, a dazzling ballhandler, and one of the best shooting guards in Sharman, plus one of the toughest players in the league, brought to the team the previous fall in a relatively unheralded deal, Bob Brannum. Basketball was and is a contact sport, and in the 1950s, Auerbach fielded a team that personified his own feistiness, the gracelessness that compelled him to light a cigar as his team wrapped up another victory or caused him to blow smoke into the faces of many unfortunates who crossed him.

Having purchased Brannum's contract from the Sheboygan Redskins in September 1950, Auerbach unleashed him on his opponents for the next four years, three of which Brannum finished within the top six league-wide for fouls, not bad for a part-time player who never scored more than 500 points in any of his four seasons in Boston.

His pedigree suggested otherwise. The twin brother of Clarence Brannum, Bob starred for Adolph Rupp's dominant Kentucky teams, earning All-American honors for the 1943–44 season before departing for the war. After serving his country, he found that Rupp had different plans for him, having fallen in love with Alex Groza and Ralph Beard; Rupp deliberately humiliated Brannum, even separating him from his teammates in their dorm. Brannum transferred to Michigan State, where he played the game of his career against the Wildcats, dominating his former teammates as the Spartans lost by only two. This was the year that Kentucky won the SEC conference title, the NCAA title, and the Olympic gold medal, though their later involvement in a point-shaving scandal enveloped Groza and Beard.

Per his daughter Debbie, "A boring game was when Daddy didn't get into a fight, and I was thrilled when he'd get in a fight. I'd love it when he'd come home with stitches in his forehead." He kept Bob Cousy in one piece.

Bob Donham provided quality play off the bench, paving the way for the "sixth man" concept Red Auerbach employed so effectively after Frank Ramsey joined the team. Odd thing about Donham: his field goal percentage generally hovered around .500, not bad for the time, but his free throw percentage also ended in the same level, as he shot .507 at the charity stripe. Even Dennis Rodman, Wilt Chamberlain, and Shaquille O'Neal shot with more accuracy from the line. In 1951–52, Donham exceeded both Bob Cousy and Bill Sharman by almost 100 percentage points and Ed Macauley by about 50 percentage points from the floor, but he ran out of luck when an opponent wisely fouled him. Fortunately, Boston also has two players in the all-time list for percentage of free throws made, Ray Allen and Larry Bird, with Bill Sharman occupying the 12th spot.

Brannum and another newcomer, Bob Harris, brought some muscle up front, but the problem of Ed Macauley, a terrific outside shooter miscast as a center, remained. Georgetown's John Mahnken tried to help, but then the team gave up a lot on offense. Cousy starred at guard and Bill Sharman proved a fast learner, while Chuck Cooper started at forward and Bob Donham gave the team almost 2,000 minutes off the bench.

The Celtics continued to spend their preseason basically as a barnstorming team throughout the Middlesex villages and towns of New England, places so remote that Paul Revere and his horse Lucky could not have navigated there, even in the mid-20th century. Nobody wanted to ride with Auerbach, a man who loved to speed his way through poorly constructed and treacherous rural roads. One day Cousy and some teammates had gotten a head start on Red and stopped at the side of the road to relieve themselves. Up came Red, asking what they were doing. Rather than own up, they told him they had run out of gas. Off went Red to the nearest service station to load up on a can of gas so they would make the game. When he got there, he noticed that Cousy and the men had lied to him, as they raced away from Red to the upcoming game, waving and laughing at him. That might have been the only time any player beat Red to a game.

After the season began, the Celtics roared past virtually everybody, winning nine of their first 11 games, losing only to the Knicks and the Syracuse Nationals, two teams that gave Red fits in pre–Elvis Presley era America. They finished the season second in the Eastern Division, slated to play the Knicks again in the first round of the playoffs.

One of the more interesting events ever held at the old Boston Garden was the Milkman's Special, a midnight contest between the Celtics and the Fort Wayne Pistons on February 21, 1952. Supposedly a scheduling snafu precipitated this strange scheduling, as Walter Brown's Ice Capades were already booked for the Garden on that date. In any event, few milkmen or anyone else attended the game, a Celtics blowout of the Pistons. They never tried this again.

Unlike the previous campaign, the Celtics won their first game against the Knicks, their first playoff victory since Honey Russell's charges defeated the Stags in their second year. Cousy led all scorers with 31 points, but five other Celtics players—Cooper, Sharman, Donham, Macauley, and Harris—scored in double figures, as the Celtics won 105–94.

Now the bad news: Bill Sharman, after leading a balanced attack in the first game, contracted chicken pox, quite a serious matter for an adult, and he recuperated for the remainder of the series. Without Sharman, the Celtics lost two close ones 101–97 and 88–87, dependent almost solely on Macauley and Cousy for scoring.

Controversy erupted over the officiating, particularly in the final match, a loss in double overtime. With time running out in the second OT, behind by one point, former Celtic George Kaftan took the Knicks' inbound pass, then froze the ball around center court. Down to his last seconds he passed to teammate Ernie Vandeweghe, guarded at the foul line by Boston's only rookie, Dick Dickey. Vandeweghe attempted a hook shot, and the referees called Dickey with either a cheap foul at best, a phantom call at worst. Vandeweghe made both free throws, eliminating the Celtics from the playoffs.

Apoplectically, Auerbach assailed commissioner Maurice Podoloff and a congregation of the referees on the way into the dressing room, roaring, "Great job. Wonderful work on the officials. Hope you guys can sleep nights."

Auerbach castigating the referees happened all of the time, but there was a certain stink surrounding the officiating in this last game. Earlier, a ref had instructed Bob Donham to stand back, and when Donham commented, "I'm on the free throw line," he incurred a technical. Later, for this first and only time all season, Easy Ed Macauley fouled out. Cousy fouled out too, and when he walked off the court, the New York crowd burst into cheers of appreciation for this foe, a man who carried his team all three games and running the backcourt in the last two games without Sharman.

So in the final moments of the penultimate game, the Celtics lacked Sharman, Macauley, and Cousy while their only rookie, Dick Dickey, defended a much better player than himself, Kiki Vandeweghe's dad. In a postgame interview, Vandeweghe admitted that the play had been drawn up that way: "We played for me to get the final shot because I had a height advantage on Dickey." It did not seem fair.

In the locker room, Dickey responded, shouting, "I knew they were going to do it...but I didn't foul him!" Hardly more composed, Walter Brown groused, "New York teams are always well protected in this league." Troubling officiating aside, New York advanced, and the Celtics returned to their normal lives, Brannum as a golf pro, Harris to his job in Indiana, Macauley to do radio work back in St. Louis, and Sharman to the Brooklyn Dodgers farm system, where ominously it was reported, "[I]t is doubtful if this talented forward will return to basketball next season."

Red Auerbach gobbled Chinese food and cigars and plotted his revenge.

chapter 8
Overpriced Stars

1952–53

In the next NBA draft, the Celtics bombed out on almost all of their picks, but then so did pretty much every other team, with the Lakers getting the only truly talented player, Clyde Lovellette, a future four-time All-Star and at career's end, a Celtic. Interestingly enough, Boston drafted its best player in the 10th round, Gene Conley, one of the most interesting characters in sports history.

A two-sport star, Gene Conley took a hiatus from basketball after his first season with the Celtics to devote himself to a major league baseball career as a pitcher. Experiencing much more success on the diamond than Bill Sharman had, he suited up for four All-Star Games as a member of the Braves and the Phillies. Conley ended his pitching career with the Red Sox, where he gained his greatest fame by jumping off a team bus with Pumpsie Green and leaving the team for a lost weekend, attempting at one point to jump on a flight to Israel. A sheepish Conley later rejoined the Sox after engaging in a talk with team owner Tom Yawkey about minimal behavior expected of a professional.

The Celtics had one of the best records in the NBA this season, two games off the eventual champion Lakers, a hollow statistic because Boston won only one of the six games it played against Minneapolis, as George Mikan dominated at center. Again, despite their impressive 46–25 record, the Celtics landed third in the Eastern Division.

In the playoffs, they faced Dolph Schayes and the Syracuse Nationals, with the Celtics winning the first game in balanced fashion, after which the clubs traveled to Boston for one of the Celtics' most notable games to this day. This is where it got really nasty.

Held at the Boston Garden, this second game proved most chippy, a four-overtime event. The Celtics scored more points via free throws than field goals, an epic event that the Greek poet Homer might have appreciated, assuming he did not have obstructed seats.

This was no boring game where the opponents traded baskets all night, as Bob Brannum physically assaulted Dolph Schayes all evening, restricting him to eight points. The Boston police department officers and Celtics ushers at one point interceded to break up a fight between Schayes and Brannum as the referees blew the whistle for a total of 107 fouls.

Meanwhile, Bob Cousy resembled Achilles without the flaw as he scored 50 points, hitting crucial free throws, making 30, missing only two, while getting hacked continuously. Brannum, in between felling bodies left and right, appreciated his teammate's performance, the "greatest thing anybody ever saw." At the end, only Boston stood, 111–105 victors as Red Auerbach "nearly lighted his nose instead of a cigar," proudly observing, "Cousy, you ask? Don't get me started. I could go all night on what that kid did. He's only the best."

The Boston Celtics had won their first playoff series ever.

Then they lost in four to the Knicks. Maybe Boston had given too much in that last game against the Nationals, or perhaps the Knickerbockers coach, Joe Lapchick, a pretty wily guy, had just digested Auerbach's game plan and knew he had to fight fire with fire. Lapchick did not let his big men get thrown about, and the Celtics still relied too much on the trio of Cousy, Sharman, and Macauley for points. With that, a very good and spirited Boston Celtic campaign ended.

1953–54

During this era of good feeling, Walter Brown graciously hosted the NBA meetings in Boston for three days in late April 1953. Across town, Auerbach charmed a crowd of 600 guests at the annual Boot and Shoe dinner at the Sheraton. Subbing for Cousy, Red deadpanned, "This is the worst substitution I ever made, myself for Bob Cousy." He promised the crowd he meant to choose a corner man in the upcoming draft, and the club reaped its best haul ever, gaining Frank Ramsey in the first round and later Cliff Hagan and Lou Tsioropoulos. All three had graduated from Kentucky, but due to the point-shaving scandal that earlier had enveloped the program, they played another year in college rather than joining the NBA for 1953–54. The Hagan pick ultimately helped form the cornerstone of the Celtics dynasty.

Sports Illustrated once marveled at the ability of sixth man Frank Ramsey to run onto a court and either immediately score or draw a foul, describing him as "a rangy, easy-mannered, crew-cut 6'3", [who] apparently accomplishes his two special feats because of an unusually deceptive court style. He pads along the floor, barely raising his knees from a horizontal plane, skimming the surface like a gull over water, seemingly bemused and sleepy-eyed. Then, without changing expression or otherwise betraying the extra effort going into each stride, he shifts into high gear, quickly pulls ahead of the man guarding him, and is in the clear for a long pass (generally from Cousy) and a layup." In the same article, Bill Russell tells the story when "One time…Frank came into the game and he got to the free throw line so quickly that he was too 'cold' to take his shot. He had to warm up before shooting."

Otherwise, the club packaged four players and, most important, cash for All-Star Don Barksdale of the strapped Baltimore Bullets franchise. When contacted about the transaction, Barksdale prefaced his statement by saying nice things about the Celtics but intimating that he might not play basketball anymore, though he did fortunately change his mind.

Avoiding the Festivus rush, Walter Brown aired his grievances against his ballplayers publicly after they lost three of the first four games of the new season, stating, "I have three players getting more money than the entire Philadelphia team, but all they're doing is reading their press clippings.… I can lose just as easily with a cheap ballclub." Auerbach had seen his owner earlier in a heightened level of exasperation, so rather than try to stem the tide, he heaped on the abuse to an eager crowd of media at the luncheon at the Lenox Hotel.

In the distant shire town of Worcester, Bob Cousy learned of the remarks, so he requested some air time in a local radio station and called out his employer and coach, reasoning that if they felt so strongly, they should trade him. A summit followed in Boston, after which the story died, but Brown's outburst reflected the frustration shared by management, players, and fans alike, a feeling that only a dominant pivot player could assuage.

And to think, it had been such a serene off-season.

Walter Brown hired Johnny Most to replace Curt Gowdy for Celtics broadcasts staring in 1953. Introducing Johnny Most to any Celts follower seems redundant. Johnny passed more than 20 years ago and retired a few years before he died. Thousands of new fans have grown up without the singular experience of having Johnny call the games "from high about courtside." Best known for his call "Havlicek stole the ball!" in the Eastern Division Finals in 1965, that might not have been his best quote. During a game against the Warriors in the mid-1970s, an opposing fan threw a potato at either the Celtics bench or Most, missing both. Afterward, Johnny Most, in his gravelly voice rhetorically considered a philosophical problem that had dogged mankind since the feeding of the Christians to the lions at the Roman Coliseum: "What kind of nut would bring a potato to a game?"

Back then, announcers traveled with the team, and Most became even more of a homer than he might normally because he played cards, shared jokes, and became friends with the players, and in this season the club played in some bizarre locales. They played the Bullets in New Haven, Connecticut; the Lakers in New York City; the Philadelphia Warriors in Milwaukee; and the Milwaukee Hawks in Baltimore.

Speaking of the Hawks, in late November, Red Auerbach packaged together five players no one heard of in exchange for Jack Nichols, their power forward, one of the shrewdest deals the club ever consummated. Milwaukee really got consummated, as none of the five ex-Celts collectively played as much as a nanosecond in the NBA. Nichols' presence probably also foretold the end of Chuck Cooper's time in Boston, as Red became increasingly impatient with his lack of rebounding and perceived lack of desire.

The NBA produced a most unusual playoff scenario for the opening round at season's end, a round-robin tournament; Boston advanced by dint of winning both games against the Knicks, though the Celtics lost both games to Syracuse. All this accomplished was the elimination of the Knicks. In the next "round," Boston faced Syracuse, where they lost both games to the Nationals, ending Boston's season.

The predictable demise of the Celtics in the spring of 1954 caused Walter Brown to engage in another blowup, accusing the players of quitting and questioning the propriety of retaining the head coach. Brown cooled off, as he always did, but reportedly Auerbach took a pay cut to stay on as coach.

In the draft, he picked Holy Cross star Togo Palazzi and Red Morrison in the second round and then chose a bunch of other players who never suited up for them.

Perhaps Easy Ed Macauley lacked the strength to consistently post low, but Bob Cousy had an interesting take, which he shared in an interview several years later. He said initially Macauley scored well driving to the basket and scoring in the post but altered his game over time. Defensively, Macauley devoted himself to covering his own man, even when a teammate needed help. In contrast, Cousy stated that Bill Russell always came over to help a teammate on defense.

Either way, without a strong pivoting presence, this remained a team capable of playing in the postseason, just not for a very long period of time.

chapter 9

A Player Away

1954–55

Frustrated with constantly losing early in the playoffs, the 1954–55
Celtics rewarded Red Auerbach with his worst record in Boston, 36–36,
despite the presence of four future Hall of Famers (six, if you include
Auerbach and Don Barksdale, inducted as a contributor). It is a difficult
team to fathom—Don Barksdale played well but considered quitting
due to not playing enough and Chuck Cooper slid further down the
bench, but the club still had Bob Cousy, Ed Macauley, and Bill Sharman.
Frank Ramsey played very well as a rookie, as did Jack Nichols and Bob
Brannum off the bench.

The institution of the shot clock seemingly should have rewarded
Boston, with Cousy whipping down the floor, but fast breaks started
with good rebounding, a trait the team did not possess.

Despite this mediocre showing, they defeated the Knicks in the
first round of the playoffs. Predictably, Cousy, Macauley, Sharman, and
Ramsey accounted for most of the points scored, though Jack Nichols
ran up 22 to lead his team to the rubber match win. Then they advanced
to Syracuse, where the Nationals dispatched them with embarrassing
ease. Counting the regular season, the semifinals, and Eastern Division
Finals, Boston lost one more game than the team won that year.

Worcester has witnessed far too many tragedies involving the dedicated members
of its fire department. During the summer of 1955, Bob Cousy conceived and
organized a basketball game to benefit the widows of two firefighters who had lost
their lives, raising the then very significant sum of $4,000.

Financially, Walter Brown and Lou Pieri began to make money and the sport had certainly grown in popularity, but little else distinguishes this dull season in Boston.

1955–56

In the 1955–56 season, Boston lost right away as Frank Ramsey had to sit out the year to fulfill his military obligation. Auerbach fiscally fleeced the Rochester Royals out of their four-time All-Star and future Hall of Fame center Arnie Risen for cash only. Red liked Risen's game; he was a strong guy who racked up a ton of fouls but took a batch of foul shots on the other end and rebounded. The cash-strapped Royals became to Boston what the Kansas City Athletics had become to the New York Yankees, a team that gave away its best players for relatively nothing in return.

Jim Loscutoff took over Bob Brannum's role as chief enforcer and guard for star guard Bob Cousy, but little else changed. The team played well enough during the regular season, certainly improved since its last edition, but then exited quickly in the playoffs as was their custom, this time to the Syracuse Nationals.

After the Celtics endured a particularly bruising loss to the Lakers, in which Boston shot a then-record 56 of 66 free throw attempts, they picked up Bob Houbregs in a dispersal draft (the Bullets folded following the 14th game of the season). He played very briefly with the Celtics, cut before the NBA teams had to get their rosters down to 10 players. He did have a memorable conversation with Walter Brown though, relating long after the event, "Anyway, this gentleman walks toward me, stops, and says, 'Excuse me. My name is Walter Brown, and I'd like to tell you a story. We tried to buy your father in 1929. But the stock market crashed and after that we could get anybody we wanted for nothing.'" An old hockey man, Brown referred to Houbregs' father, John, who lost an eye to the sport, making Bob Houbregs' decision to play basketball so much easier.

Many Celtics fans wrongfully assume that Red Auerbach served as their first coach and his charges always won championships until he retired, but probably even more chuckle, believing that Red became only a genius when Bill Russell started his tenure in Boston. The first misconception is patently incorrect, but the second viewpoint ignores just how close the Celtics came to winning during each of Red's first years leading them.

Problem was, though Auerbach had some terrific shooters, he possessed not one stand-out rebounder. In the first six Red years, Boston did not have a single man in the top five in rebounds per game or total rebounds ever, this in a league that ranged from only eight to 11 teams, depending on how many franchises folded in this span. And it's not like the club did not perceive the defect; it tried to fatten up Easy Ed Macauley, but he was the type of guy who could eat a dozen donuts per day and lose weight. So although Boston won some playoff games and series, the Celtics never finished first in the Eastern Division, nor did they participate in the NBA Finals.

Some perspective might help. John Havlicek is one of the greatest basketball players in history, and when you mention his name, his shooting, endurance, longevity, leadership, clutch play, and versatility all come to mind but not necessarily his rebounding. That shocks no one, because as a swingman, it was not his role to crash the boards, particularly when you have Bill Russell or, later, Dave Cowens and Paul Silas as teammates. Yet in his twenties, Havlicek matches up pretty well in the rebounding department with Macauley, a much taller center.

The easy answer as to the Celtics' relative lack of success that no one will ever challenge you on is "They didn't have Russell yet, stupid!" You will win every bar argument with that simple rejoinder but maybe you shouldn't, because the Celtics should have advanced much further in the playoffs than they did. There was a parity in the top three in their division every year, except the time the Celts went .500, even with a great coach with a well-conditioned team. They had the advantage over their counterparts approaching the playoffs.

And they had better players. The Knicks, like the Nationals, had two stars in Dick McGuire and Dolph Schayes, respectively, but most of their supporting casts were peopled with very good players. Meanwhile, the

Celtics trotted out four Hall of Famers: Cousy, Macauley, and then later Bill Sharman and Frank Ramsey.

True, they lacked the dominant center prototype of the era, but players such as Harris, Brannum, and Loscutoff gave opposing centers the fits quite often, yet they never even had the chance to play in a championship series. Lacking a decent rebounder, the players had to work much harder than their opponents to win, a taxing demand over the course of a season.

Truth is, Boston probably should have played in two or three NBA championship series and maybe stolen at least one during those years. Maybe if they had had a rebounder who did nothing else well, the Celtics might have done so, but they always came up short. Always.

Upset but determined, Auerbach had already seen the future of professional basketball, William Fenton Russell. And Red Auerbach meant to get him.

chapter 10

Rookie of the Year

Red Auerbach had worked on this one, sensing that Bill Russell personified the type of tough defense and rebounding necessary to finally net the Celtics a title. Trouble was, Boston had a low pick in the draft, with the Rochester Royals up first, followed by the St. Louis Hawks. Walter Brown had experienced financial hardship, most notably in his first four years with the Celtics, and he correctly believed that Rochester needed "Mr. Green" (cash) to keep it alive as a franchise. So Walter Brown offered Rochester an extended run by the Ice Capades, an extremely popular attraction of the day and owned by Brown, in exchange for the Royals passing on Russell. So Rochester got Mr. Green and chose Duquesne's guard, Sihugo Green, as the first overall pick in the draft. Phase One, and Brown and Auerbach had gotten their oats. So far.

Predictably, St. Louis chose Bill Russell with the second overall pick, but a deal had already occurred whereby Boston traded Ed Macauley and the rights to Cliff Hagan for Russell. The deal worked out well for both clubs: the Hawks received two Hall of Famers to augment the superb Bob Pettit, eventually earning their one and only NBA crown in 1958; and the Celtics obtained the greatest basketball player ever to that time. On a more altruistic note, Ed Macauley at the time had a sick son and wanted to be with him in their hometown of St. Louis as much as possible, so the trade worked out on humanitarian grounds, too. Too bad Easy Ed had not been born later—a tall, thin guy who never ventured into the paint and excelled at swishing 15 footers. The 2012–13 edition of the Celtics hoarded players like he was.

One last hurdle to clear—Boston had to obtain a league exemption to the rule that prohibited a team from trading away its first draft choice.

Though impossible to summarize Bill Russell's career here, consider this: 13 seasons, 12 All-Star appearances, 11 championships, and five MVP Awards.

One can almost see and hear Walter Brown going crazy about this: "What now, I thought we had cleared the whole thing up!" The Celtics had, the league consented, and by April's end a permanent rainbow hovered about the gritty old Garden.

The other draft selections, Holy Cross' Tommy Heinsohn and Russell's roommate at the University of San Francisco, K.C. Jones, wrapped up a day when the Celtics chose three future Hall of Famers. Now the club had the greatest center of all time, a six-time All-Star power forward, and a point guard whose fingers eventually accumulated championship rings both as a player and head coach.

By May Day, the time when the old Soviet Union staged boring parades with big tanks and larger missiles, the Celtics had the nastiest lineup on the planet. Arnie Risen started at center until Russell joined the team after the Olympics. At guard, Bob Cousy and Bill Sharman continued to share the backcourt while Jim Loscutoff, Jack Nichols, Dick Hemric, and Lou Tsioropoulos joined Heinsohn at forward, with sixth man extraordinaire Frank Ramsey coming in to polish off the opposition.

At summer's end, Auerbach also picked future Hall of Famer Andy Phillip off waivers, giving him six future Hall of Famers to call on in the upcoming season. They would have had seven, but K.C. Jones went to the military (then briefly to the NFL's Los Angeles Rams for a tryout), until he rediscovered his true calling a couple years later.

One overlooked key to the Celtics mystique? Athleticism. Not only did they sign up some of the finest basketball players ever, they also boasted a number of multisport stars. Chuck Connors, Gene Conley, Danny Ainge, and Bill Sharman played major league baseball, K.C. Jones and John Havlicek tried out for NFL teams, and Don Eliason played two years in the NFL and Hal Crisler played for five. After he was cut, the team's first draft choice in 1981, Charles Bradley, tried out for an NFL team. John Simmons reportedly played some pro baseball. Another factor is intelligence; like later legendary local coach Bill Belichick, Red Auerbach did not suffer fools much. Although Auerbach did not design hundreds of plays, one more complicated than the next, he wanted mentally quick athletes, and he made certain to get them.

Understandably, the club started a bit slowly at 3–3 as this radically new team gelled; then they defeated the Royals on November 17, the start of a 10-game winning streak. After reaching that goal, the Celtics won 20 games before any other club, all of this before Russell joined the team. This is a good time to stress the importance of the addition of Tommy Heinsohn to the Celtics. Because he played a full season in Boston his first year while Russell joined late due to his obligations to the Olympics (the basketball event occurred in late autumn), he earned Rookie of the Year honors. Heinsohn was a deserving candidate, a star in any era of the sport. Perhaps Celtics fans, even those who saw him play, have become too accustomed to thinking of him as the beefy broadcaster, parceling out "Tommy Points" to those deserving Celtics candidates who play hard and particularly smart.

Watch some old film—this was one athletic forward with a nice shooting touch. And tough, finishing third that first year in fouls, but again, this was not a goofy, clumsy Samurai Belushi caricature slamming people in the paint. He ended up fourth that year in defensive win shares (the Royals' Maurice Stokes finished first, with the top five rounded out by Celtics Cousy, Russell, and Loscutoff). A model of consistency, Heinsohn also finished 12th league-wide in all of these categories: points, points per game, total rebounds, rebounds per game, and free throw percentage. He exploited a wonderful hook shot from all distances and angles.

He did tend to shoot the ball too much—the standard joke revolved around the question, when did Tommy Heinsohn shoot the ball? Answer: when it was passed to him. Over time he improved in this area and became a much more discerning shooter, but give the guy a break; he was still winded from his four undergraduate years walking up and down the Worcester hills at Holy Cross while chain-smoking cigarettes. And he excelled in the playoffs.

Want another telling statistic? Basketball-Reference.com has a stat for all-time Hall of Fame Probability. The top nine are all 1,000 percenters: Russell, Wilt Chamberlain, Kareem Abdul-Jabbar, Michael Jordan, John Havlicek, Kobe Bryant, Cousy, Magic Johnson, and Shaquille O'Neal. Tenth is Larry Bird (how is he not 1,000 percent?), and 19th is Tommy

Heinsohn. Skeptical of statistics? Bill Russell once said something to the effect that Heinsohn could play better than Bob Pettit and he could have even exceeded Elgin Baylor on the court.

Indeed, during his first regular season, the Celtics had a better regular season winning percentage *without* Russell than with him. This is not a knock on Russell; he had won a bunch of championships, traveled the world for the Olympics, and did not even get a preseason to train with his Celtics teammates. It only accentuates what a positive influence Tommy Heinsohn had on his teammates, as they glided to their first Eastern Division crown. Sufficient superlatives exist to describe Heinsohn's game and influence on the Celtics; they simply have not been used enough.

Necessity mothered the invention of Tommy Heinsohn's "no-arc jump shots and hook shots," due to the low ceiling at his hometown's half-court gym. He also might have been the only player to develop issues with Red Auerbach before becoming a Celtic. While at Holy Cross, Heinsohn was scouted at a game by Auerbach, and when Red was asked about the Crusader star, he opined that Heinsohn would never play for him because he had too much baby fat. When Heinsohn saw the quote in the newspapers, he phoned Auerbach and let him have it. Auerbach did not take it personally, as he drafted Heinsohn and then promptly ran 20 pounds of gristle off of him at practice.

And now Russell! Russell joined the team on December 22, 1956, a classic two-point victory over the Hawks, and Banner Fever gripped the Hub. More than 11,000 fans bought tickets for the game, a huge crowd for the time. To make room on the roster for Russ, the Celts let go of popular Togo Palazzi, selling him to Syracuse, where he thrived for the next few years.

Russell had experienced an exhilarating year: his (and K.C.'s) San Francisco Dons won the NCAA championship, he led the United States to an Olympic gold medal, and then he founded a professional dynasty. Plus, he had to squeeze in a honeymoon between the Olympics and his first professional game. Then the nail-biting began.

Worrywarts began experiencing heightened indigestion when Boston endured a bit of a slump as the regular season whittled away, due partly to injuries. Ironman Bob Cousy missed his first full game after playing in the past 485, and the condition of his right knee remained a distraction heading into the playoffs, though Bill Sharman and Russell in particular played exceptionally well in Cousy's absence.

Bill Russell, Tommy Heinsohn, and K.C. Jones might not have been the most intriguing Celts chosen on that fateful final day in April. In the fourth round, Red Auerbach picked Dan Swartz, a small forward from Morehead State. Swartz passed on the NBA, choosing to play at the AAU level and with the National Industrial Basketball League. The NIBL's best-known player probably is Bobby Plump, a player on the high school team that served as the inspiration for the film *Hoosiers*. Red certainly did not hold it against Swartz, later choosing him to play on his 1962–63 squad, where Swartz earned a championship ring.

In the past, the Celtics had always tripped up early in the playoffs, but this time they swept the Syracuse Nationals, blowing them out of the water before facing the St. Louis Hawks in the NBA Finals.

St. Louis was a tough bunch. Owner Ben Kerner had a bulbous nose, wore loud clothes, and absolutely hated Auerbach (who had once coached his Blackhawks). The team's player/coach, Alex Hannum, was tough as nails, one of only two NBA players ever to incur seven fouls in one game (against the Celtics, of course; Don Otten is the other player who achieved this distinction). Some familiar names graced the Hawks lineup, including Easy Ed Macauley, Chuck Share (whom Auerbach drafted instead of Cousy), and Cliff Hagan, the future Hall of Famer used to obtain Bill Russell. Add future Hall of Famers Slater Martin and Bob Pettit, one of the greatest forwards in history, and the Hawks had a superb team, one that got only better thanks to some shrewd moves in the second half of the season.

Bill Russell was ranked the seventh-greatest high jumper in the world in 1956, having once jumped over 6'9", but besides his leaping prowess, one will constantly hear that he made these incredible defensive plays, seemingly "coming out of nowhere." It sounds clichéd and meaningless, but it helped to grow up in an era where television sports camera work was developing and home televisions stunk, filled with static and horizontal lines constantly moving up and down the screen. There would be a camera shot of a Celtics opponent catching an outlet pass with Bill Russell on the other side of the court, well outside the play. The cameraman would continue to focus on the dribbler with Russell presumably completely out of it, content to let his opponent net an easy layup. Then Russell, having run full blast down the court would "come out of nowhere" to block the shot of the shocked opponent.

There are more iconic pictures of Bill Russell, but perhaps none demonstrate his dedication to the team concept more than this, as he leaps over the back of an opponent to assist a fellow Celtic under the basket.

The teams split the first two games of the series, shifting the action to the third game at the Kiel Auditorium in St. Louis. Even before game time, Auerbach took the gloves off, or never put them on, as it transpired. He believed that his old friend Kerner had given the Celtics crappy balls to warm up with and then suspected the nets were not regulation height. The referees checked them (they were okay) and Kerner growled out choice epithets, enunciating his opinion in tones louder than his clothes, so Red naturally ran over to his old boss and socked him in the face.

This all occurred before the first tip!

Old Ben probably had it coming; in pre–Bobby Knight days, he had once thrown a chair at a referee, and Bill Letwin, a sportswriter for the old *Milwaukee Journal*, once described a typical game performance by

From agony to ecstasy: here Celtics rookie forward Tommy Heinsohn covers his face in Game 7 of the 1956–57 Finals against the St. Louis Hawks. But in a few moments he'll celebrate his club's first NBA title.

Kerner thusly: "When the going gets hot, he sheds his jacket. His tie and his shirt part company. His hair is mussed up. He agonizes with every shot. He raves at the officials, rides the opposition, and stews when his own players make mistakes."

Unfortunately, the Celtics lost that game by two points, necessitating winning two of the next three to force a Game 7, which they did, with Heinsohn popping in shots like he had played in the NBA for 10 years.

Fortunately the Celtics played this seventh game at the Garden, because they needed every dead spot on the parquet they might wring out of their home-court advantage, as Bob Cousy and Bill Sharman uncharacteristically both lost their shots that day. Enter Tommy Heinsohn, who scored 37 points, poised as ever, while Bill Russell scored 19 and pulled down 32 boards, blocking shots and blocking out opposing players.

In a signature moment, Bill Russell picked himself off the floor behind the Hawks' net, went the length of the floor to chase a pass by the Hawks' Jack Coleman, and then blocked the shot to send the game into overtime.

In fact, a game like this one needed two OTs. Heinsohn (along with Arnie Risen) fouled out, sitting alone on the bench with a warm-up jacket shrouding his eyes. He thought he had blown it.

Up stepped his teammates—Frank Ramsey making key foul shots, Russell blocking a shot by the Hawks' Med Park, and, after Alex Hannum leveled Loscutoff, Loscy calmly converting on both free throws. With time expiring, Hannum whipped the ball nearly the length of the floor to Bob Pettit, who missed his shot at the buzzer.

The Celtics were champions for the first time ever.

chapter 11
Bank Shots and Talking Knees

1957–58

By this time old Celtics friend Bones McKinney had entered his newest vocation, coaching the Wake Forest University basketball team. Bones knew players but always knew himself better—he once seat-belted himself to the bench so that he would not accost a ref and incur a technical foul.

Red Auerbach, during his stint at Duke as an assistant, had scouted a bit for the Celtics, and now he asked Bones to do the same, particularly as he had heard great things about a player down South. McKinney called back to provide a very negative review of that collegian but then urged Red very strongly to choose a guard from tiny North Carolina Central University.

So Red scrawled the name down on a scrap of paper and promptly lost it amid the utter clutter on his desk. On draft day, April 17, 1957, the Celtics coach feverishly shuffled papers around to find the name of that guard that Bones had raved about so much. Finally, he dug it out and, in typical Auerbach fashion, barked out like he owned the world, "The Boston Celtics choose Sam Jones."

Other than the addition of Sam Jones, Red kept a pat hand, subtracting from his roster only Dick Hemric, the former Demon Deacons power forward who, to the present day, still holds the all-time ACC record for rebounds.

Injuries nagged the team all year, most significantly Jim Loscutoff's balky knee, which caused him to shut it down after only five games and opt for surgery. No one played every game in that season, but this fact did little to deter the club from leading the NBA with total wins, eight more than Syracuse and St. Louis.

Sam Jones is renowned for his bank shots, geometric beauties designed to bounce off a backboard and into the basket, a largely lost art in the Top 10 Plays of the Day era. Such a talent seemingly could be used for other purposes, such as willing stripes and solids into corner pockets in pool, but it does not appear that Sam Jones possessed such superpowers, although apparently he never lost a game of hearts. Like Bill Sharman, he did it all.

Indeed, the Celtics did not lose until the 15th game of the season, a matchup against the Knicks in "neutral" Philadelphia. League MVP Bill Russell led the NBA in rebounds, helped out teammates on defense, and ignited the newfound Celtics' fast break, while contributing 16.6 points per game. Frank Ramsey more than doubled his minutes played and nearly tripled his scoring from the previous season, and Tommy Heinsohn continued to improve on defense while landing in the top 10 for field goals made. The Celtics still had the best backcourt in the league, if not the deepest bench, as they cruised to the Eastern Division lead, eight games ahead of Syracuse. The good luck and stellar play continued through the first round of the playoffs, which provided few challenges as they sliced through Philadelphia in five games.

In the NBA Finals, they faced the Hawks again and lost the first game by two points at the Garden. No problem—in the next game Boston blew them out 136–112 as seven Celtics scored in double figures. Team owner Walter Brown superstitiously refused to attend road games, afraid that his presence "hexed" the team, but for Game 3 at the Kiel Auditorium in St. Louis, he broke his custom. Then in that third game—third quarter, third minute—Bill Russell injured his right ankle, coming down hard after the ref called him for goaltending, immediately confirming Walter Brown's worst fear. Gamely, Russell attempted to come back later, to no avail—no wonder because he had suffered a severe strain. Without their great center (and with the Celts abominably missing 22 foul shots), Boston lost that third game by three points despite the best efforts of Frank Ramsey and Bill Sharman. Team doctor Edward Browne pronounced that Russell "had played his last basketball game of the season." Characteristically, his patient disagreed.

Jim Loscutoff was one of the toughest players in professional sports history, a role he relished. "Nobody had to ask me to do anything," he said. "In fact, Red used to have fun with me in a special drill to build my confidence after I'd had a knee operation. He'd throw a ball out on the court and say 'Go get it,' and I'd have to go diving and rolling on the floor. This was during exhibition season. Red would get the guys from the other team and say, 'Watch this,' roll out the balls for me, and I'd go diving." ESPN once ranked Loscy ninth all time for dirtiest professional team players, one place ahead of the notorious Jack "They Call Me Assassin" Tatum.

Jim Loscutoff's nickname hangs from the Garden rafters, along with the retired numbers of other Celtics legends. In a classy gesture, he later gave Dave Cowens his blessing to wear No. 18 and was rewarded by watching someone who shared his will to win wear his old number.

Stuck in St. Louis for the fourth game, Bob Cousy looked doubtful, having sustained a foot injury that necessitated a trip to the local hospital. But the Cooz did suit up and, despite having his nose bashed in the first period, he played all but 28 seconds to lead a slower-paced Celtics to victory with 24 points, tying the series 2–2. Tommy Heinsohn played his usual tough defense, holding the Hawks' Bob Pettit to 12 points.

It just kept getting worse for Russell—on April 5 his home was broken into. This act by a moron or morons cost Russell an estimated $1,300 in losses, a considerable liability then, and also contributed to his souring on many of the local fans. Despite Frank Ramsey's 30 points and a surge by the Celtics in the fourth quarter, they lost the fifth game by two points at the Garden and faced elimination as the teams returned to St. Louis.

As another demonstration of Russell's greatness, he willed himself to return for the sixth game, despite doctor's orders to the contrary, with cowbells conspiring with the cheers back at the Kiel to create a singularly hostile environment. Sharman, having sustained a right knee injury, scored 26 points, but Pettit had one of the greatest playoff games in history, scoring 50 points as the Hawks prevailed by one point and won the title. The second-best team had won, a fact made worse for Red as he saw old nemesis Ben Kerner light up a victory cigarette.

Graciously, Red stated, "I'm not criticizing anybody. I think under the conditions the boys did very well. We were not functioning at full strength, and you must be strong to knock over those Hawks." He pointed out the rash of injuries sustained by his team during the year, mentioning that he'd had a full squad for practice for only 10 games during the season and asserting, "No club in the history of the league suffered as many serious injuries as the Celtics…"

At the annual Celtics breakup dinner, veterans Andy Phillip, Arnie Risen, and Jack Nichols retired, an event that Sharman, Russell, Cousy, and Heinsohn could not attend as they headed off to an all-star series in the west.

To the date of this printing, the Hawks, whether in St. Louis or Atlanta, have never won another NBA title. It was a frustrating season in

Boston—so much had gone right until Russell hurt his ankle—but the Celtics would win again.

1958–59

There were two future Hall of Famers in the upcoming draft, Elgin Baylor and Hal Greer—and the Celtics got neither. They had no chance at Baylor, the first choice, but they unwisely chose Bennie Swain over Greer and another perennial All-Star, Wayne Embry. Repeatedly referred to by the press as a "sleeper," few people knew much about Swain before draft day. Sam Jones had played a game against him and thought Swain might become a stronger version of Dick Ricketts—the same Dick Ricketts who, after being chosen first overall in the 1955 draft, retired from basketball after three years with a .328 field goal percentage and fewer than 2,000 points (and who spent 1959 pitching for the St. Louis Cardinals). Red did spend the summer tutoring Swain in the Catskills, but the gamble failed and the sleeper slept.

Though Auerbach drafted poorly in a poor draft, K.C. Jones, fresh from a harrowing tryout with the Los Angeles Rams football team, started training with the Celtics, giving Red seven future Hall of Famers to work with, besides himself, of course. Another two-timing sports star, Gene Conley, decided to take up basketball again, spelling Russ at center. Auerbach liked him and missed him in the pre-Russell era particularly, emphasizing that "Conley made this team legitimately. We don't need him as a gate attraction; we've got the most attractive team in basketball without him. I just wish we'd had him regularly since '53. He'd be great now."

Loscy came back strong, and Sam Jones' minutes shot up dramatically. Bill Sharman set a record for free throw shooting percentage, a mark that stood for almost two decades until Rick Barry and Ernie DiGregorio made it look easy.

Behind this incredible talent and great coach, the Celtics breezed through the season, never losing more than two games in a row and finishing with a 52–20 record. They rarely scored fewer than 100 points in a game anymore, and on February 27, 1959, in a game against the Minneapolis Lakers, they went absolutely silly, winning 173–139.

Heinsohn scored 43 and Cousy put up 31 points, but it is Cousy's astonishing assist totals that distinguish him as a peerless playmaker. Never seeming to tire, he and his teammates scored 52 points in the last quarter. The Celtics eased into the Eastern Division title.

Then they almost blew it, taken to seven games in the playoff by the Syracuse Nationals, a congregation of youth (Greer, Larry Costello, and Connie Dierking), last gaspers (Dolph Schayes and Paul Seymour), and Red Kerr, who caused everyone headaches. This group limped to a 35–37 regular season record, deceptive in two respects, as the Nats picked up Hall of Fame forward George Yardley late in the season in a trade, plus they won five of their 12 games against the Celtics, never losing at home. And they became hot at precisely the right time.

In this series, George Yardley played his heart out, as did Dolph Schayes, often both of them scoring more than 30 points per night, tying the series after four games. Bob Cousy contracted a virus, returning to action after sulfa treatments restored his ambulation, but he struggled his whole time out on the court, weak as a cat. Just as he had the previous year against the Hawks, Frank Ramsey was keeping his team in games with his scoring, and Russell owned the boards. Quietly, K.C. Jones became a defensive force in this series, causing Auerbach to gush, "[Jones] did a good job."

George "Bird" Yardley was an interesting guy, a fellow who graduated from Stanford with an engineering degree and who was the first player to score 2,000 points in an NBA season. Like Bill Russell, he barfed before ballgames a lot, though Frank Ramsey attributed the Bird's success to something much more fundamental: "George had a turnaround jumper—he took it right in your face. He just jumped over you and shot like the guys do today." He hardly looked like a ballplayer, pasty-faced and prematurely balding, but after the Pistons traded him to the Nats late in the 1958–59 season, he played the last regular season games in a cast. About his early experiences in the league, he once said, "The first time around the league as a rookie, they just didn't push you around—they hit you with a clenched fist in the face." Inducted into the Hall of Fame in 1996, George Yardley lost his battle with ALS in 2004.

In the practice before the fifth game, Auerbach reamed everyone out, and it worked that one time, but in the sixth game the Nats pulled ahead in the second quarter. Boston lost any chance of a comeback after ref Sid Borgia ejected Heinsohn in the third period for unflattering remarks and Ramsey fouled out in the fourth. The hometown team won at the War Memorial to force the seventh game back in the Garden.

Bill Sharman dubbed that seventh game against Syracuse, "the greatest game of basketball I've ever seen." Ramsey, displaying perhaps the finest offensive series in NBA playoff history to that point, had to labor with a cast on his index finger yet still scored 28 points. Russell rang up 32 rebounds and 18 points while Cousy and Heinsohn also played well defensively.

Syracuse led by eight at the half and at one point, Boston had to come back from a 16-point deficit, but as he would do so often in the future for the Celtics, Sam Jones thrived under pressure, scoring 19 points, the one weapon the Nats had no answer for. Boston held on to win 130–125.

At the end, Auerbach expressed his mutual admiration for both friend and foe: "This is the greatest team ever—it didn't quit. And don't forget we beat a great team out there." Frank Ramsey, the Kentucky Colonel, played great often, and this was his finest hour.

Having survived Syracuse, the Celtics won the Finals with embarrassing ease, in four straight against the Lakers, the first of this now great rivalry. The Lakers had no business being in the championship round— they had compiled a 33–39 record during the regular season, losing to Boston every time they played. Elgin Baylor is one of the greatest players of all time and Hot Rod Hundley scored a bit, but mostly the lineup consisted of once great players in the twilight of their careers.

The Lakers tried everything, switching Hub hotels looking for better luck, but nothing worked. Even Auerbach eased up a bit before the third game at the Minneapolis Auditorium, taking his team on a shootaround for an hour, almost freezing his team in that barn. Russell imitated Cousy, and Cousy performed a passable rendition of Goose Tatum's walking dribble. As Red said, "I have to let them have a little fun, as long as no one gets hurt."

After losing the third game, Lakers coach John Kundla admitted, "Russell has our club worrying every second. It's getting so every one of the five men on the court thinks Russell is covering him on every play. I never sensed that a defensive player could mean so much to the game until Russell appeared."

Russell and his men put their opposition out of their misery in St. Paul, becoming the first NBA team to sweep the Finals. Russell grabbed 30 rebounds and played particularly well in the clutch to preserve and protect his team's lead in light of a late Lakers charge. Reserve Gene Conley scored 10 points and rebounded 10 balls himself, as Ramsey, Sharman, Cousy, and Heinsohn closed it out, lifting Auerbach onto their shoulders after the final buzzer. Then they threw Red and team trainer Buddy LeRoux into the showers.

The team flew home and received a key to the city. When asked about putting off retirement, Bob Cousy replied, "I'll have to talk to my legs all summer. I hope they say 'yes' to me."

chapter 12

Keeping Up
with the Joneses

1959–60

From 1945 to late August 1949, the United States had a monopoly over the atomic bomb, until the Soviet Union detonated a baby of its own. Likewise, for nearly three years the Boston Celtics not only had the best player but one who dominated all opponents, until the Philadelphia Warriors signed Wilt Chamberlain. It has become dogma that Chamberlain won scoring titles but Bill Russell won championships, and that is true but incomplete. Chamberlain also generally led in rebounds and minutes played—or came close in those leaguewide categories for most of his career and always showed up in shape. Never for a moment mistakenly believe that the man did not possess more talent as a basketball player than perhaps every human being not named Michael Jordan.

Defensive deficiencies, an inability to communicate with his coaches, a quirky devotion to never fouling out of a game—these tendencies became apparent later. Eventually, Red Auerbach and Bill Russell devised strategies to prevent Wilt from becoming a winner, but in the fall of 1959, Chamberlain frightened Boston fans far more than Sputnik and the Soviet Union. Chamberlain was their first confrontation with Darth Vader. He could have killed the Celtics.

Unfortunately for Wilt, he had been born half a dozen years too late. Even given his tenuous familiarity with the team concept, in the early 1950s, he, not George Mikan, would have won all of the titles just because his skill so vastly exceeded anything out there. By Wilt's rookie year, not only did the Celtics have Russell, but the Royals fielded Wayne Embry, and by the mid-1960s, he also had to post up against Willis Reed and Walt Bellamy. And by then everyone figured that if you rope-a-doped Wilt for four quarters and let him score, you still could defeat his team. Predicted Bob Cousy before Christmas, 1959, "It's only a question of time before each club will have a man to counter Chamberlain."

Still, in the fall of 1959 he scared everyone, so the Celtics had to adapt to this challenge to persist as champions. Fortunately, Cousy's legs, so tired by the playoffs, said "yes," a relief to Celtics fans. Increasingly though, Sam Jones and K.C. Jones played more minutes, a mutually beneficial development insofar as it increased the effectiveness of the older veterans to get a bit more rest. Neither the Cooz nor his teammates got any relief after training began, with the Lakers sharing the exhibitions with Boston that fall. In a creative attempt to drum up fans in Minnesota, the Celtics and the Lakers fused a doubleheader one day with the Boston Bruins and Providence Reds hockey clubs. Then came the regular season.

Red Auerbach tried out an ordained minister that year, Bart Leach, a star at Penn and previously a schoolboy basketball legend south of Boston at Fairhaven High School, where in the early 1950s he led his team to two titles and a record of 49–1. Women's basketball legend Sheila Tunstall McKenna grew up idolizing Leach, whom she called "just the nicest, best man you could ever meet." Leach did not make the final cut, probably for the best because by this time, as Bill Russell once put it in *Second Wind*, "If a bomb had blown up our road hotel on any given night, it's safe to say there'd have been a large number of extra bodies in the wreckage."

Bill Russell's rivalry with Wilt Chamberlain began this year on November 7 at the Garden, with Wilt outscoring Russell and the Celtics winning. As described in *Sports Illustrated* after, "What the duel proved, chiefly, is that against Russell, Chamberlain cannot get away with the few simple offensive moves he has found so effective against lesser men. Every time he tried to use his chief weapon, a fall-away jump shot,

Russell went up with him; Russell's large hand flicked away at his vision, slapped at the ball, once blocked it outright—a shocking experience for Wilt Chamberlain. All told, in this man-to-man situation Chamberlain hit exactly four baskets; the rest of his 30 points were made on tip-ins and a few dunk shots, in which, free of Russell, he stuffed the ball into the basket from above it." Wilt outscored Russell, but Boston won, as it largely would thereafter, by containment—exasperate the hell out of Chamberlain so that he would work that much harder to post huge individual numbers, while the Celtics team prevailed.

Chamberlain won both Rookie of the Year and MVP honors, yet Boston won its series with the Warriors that year and finished 10 games ahead of them in the standings.

Still, Boston had to face Chamberlain in the playoffs after the Warriors had beaten the Syracuse Nationals in the first round. By this time Wilt had started whining about other players shoving him around. In what became habitual, Wilt generally outscored Russell but his team generally lost, and in this fashion Boston dispensed with Philly in six games, after which Chamberlain announced his retirement from the NBA. If he only had a heart.

That left only the St. Louis Hawks to conquer. As usual, Bob Pettit and Cliff Hagan scored bushels of baskets, but this time the Celtics suffered with Bob Cousy coming out cold the first few games. The series see-sawed before the deciding seventh game at Boston Garden. As soon as Cooz found his groove, Boston simply had too many weapons for the Hawks—even K.C. Jones scored in double figures in one of the games. The Celtics outscored St. Louis by 18 points in the second quarter and then held them off with superior defense after intermission.

In defeat, Pettit praised Bill Russell to the pantheon: "I think he played today what could be called one of the truly great games of all time. He made us think every minute he was out there. He made us respect him every second of the game. And above it all, he never did anything that was wrong."

Bob Cousy slumped in the first four games of the Finals against the Hawks. Before the fifth game, Walter Brown and he attended Mass together, after which the Cooz dropped 21 points to help lead the team to victory. Grumblings from fans (and Cousy himself) that their point guard "was slipping" did not bear up to scrutiny as he led the NBA for the eighth straight year in assists with 715, his highest total ever. Cousy did not lose a step, but in the desperate last minutes of the sixth game against the Hawks, Bill Russell lost a sneaker when he ran down the length of the court to block a Cliff Hagan shot. Alertly, Sam Jones picked it up and passed it down to Russell, in order to properly equip his center for transition onto offense.

Notice that Pettit did not single out Russell for scoring (22 points) or rebounding (35), and that is why Bill Russell got all the rings and Wilt racked up the monster stats. How can you lose when your center never does anything wrong?

After their increasingly less intimate going-away party, Sam Jones signed up with the old Massachusetts District Commission to run Hyde Park's youth program at the Moynihan Playground, hoping to "sharpen [his] shooting eye and keep [his] weight down to normal." He did not play much basketball, although he did keep fit by playing a lot of tennis and even engaging in an occasional game of horseshoes. As might be expected of the master of bank shots, he once hit 18 ringers in a row.

1960–61

Red Auerbach did not know whether to get mad or get sick the first time he saw his new rookie, Thomas "Satch" Sanders, walk into camp, decked out in glasses and kneepads. Regaining his composure, Red grilled his rookie, then instructed him that glasses conveyed weakness, and knee-pads, well, they were even worse, and he had to eliminate the wardrobe malfunctions. Not trusting Satch, Red ordered a veteran to dispose of the kneepads if he ever saw them laying around the locker room.

It worked. Thomas Sanders altered his appearance to become Satch Sanders, the coolest player in the NBA. After all, he was the man who visited the White House and when he left, told president John F. Kennedy to "Take it easy, baby."

On a less fashionable note, Red instructed Satch from the first camp to forget about scoring—let Bill Sharman, Cousy, Heinsohn, and Sam Jones do that. His role was to defend. So in practice, Satch attacked Jim Loscutoff, demonstrating his toughness. He relished his role, becoming one of the NBA's best defenders of the 1960s, never scoring 1,000 points in a season, though often accumulating some of the highest annual fouls committed.

Like many African American athletes, he also experienced racism, one example being the time that he "went with Sam Jones to buy groceries for the hotel so we could save money. On the way back to the hotel local police surrounded us with guns drawn. We were scared." Scared but unbowed, Satch later became the first African American coach in the Ivy League at Harvard and then later coached the Celtics. He also developed programs at the NBA designed to help retired players make sound choices about their future. A glaring omission from the Basketball Hall of Fame in light of his excellence as a Celtic, he finally received notice of his induction as a contributor in the class of 2011.

His arrival in Boston gave Red Auerbach eight future Hall of Famers in his locker room.

One of them was named Bill Russell. In attempting to describe Russell's contribution to his team's success, it makes some sense to analyze just one aspect of what he brought to the game of basketball each year. This year he played 3,458 minutes, almost 1,000 more minutes than the teammate with the second-highest total, Bob Cousy.

Traditionally, Russell attended Celtics practices in body only, listening to Red speak at the beginning and then drinking tea and watching everyone else run the length of the court all morning. His rationale, which Auerbach did not seriously challenge, was that he needed fresh legs come game time. Usually, a boast like that by an athlete masks laziness and selfishness and results in a fine or loss of playing time. Auerbach calibrated, however, that his star center had a singular personality who rose to the occasion by following his own path, and so the coach permanently tabled the matter. Russell then went out each night and played with a savage level of intensity. His teammates loved him, and he led his team to 57 wins against 22 defeats.

Russell might have enjoyed watching practices from the bleachers with Thomas Lipton and Earl Grey, but even he had to participate in the grueling preseason scrimmages. After Auerbach completed his "daily double" practices at Babson, the team embarked on a circuit of intersquad games in Massachusetts burgs such as Bedford, Gardner, Roxbury, Brockton, and Lynn. Later the Celtics traveled around New England, played the Lakers, and then flew to the West Coast for their first ever exhibitions there.

After having drafted Jerry West, the Lakers had deserted Minnesota for Los Angeles, setting off a number of rumors. Desiring a Californian star for their relocated franchise, supposedly the Lakers ownership discussed trading West for Bill Sharman. Unfortunately those discussions did not bear fruit, though talk also centered around the Lakers recruiting Sharman as their coach. The Celtics co-opted this possibility by signing up their veteran guard. Having battened down their roster, the Celtics won the Eastern Division by 11 games.

Long forgotten, one of the club's most impressive victories occurred on March 12, 1961, in Syracuse, New York, against the Nationals, the final game of the regular season. The game meant little statistically— Boston had long since clinched the Eastern Division title—yet Red's men sent the game into overtime, eventually winning 136–134 behind Sam Jones' 44 points and Bill Russell's buzzer beater with 13 seconds left.

Formalities aside, Sam Jones had by now supplanted Sharman as the premier shooting guard, in this, Bill's final season before retiring. Sharman had lost a step, accounting for his frustration when he threw a punch in one game at Jerry West, having been beaten or faked out much of the game. Sharman missed 18 games that season, yet contributed significantly in the playoffs. Otherwise, Loscy returned from successful back surgery as the core of the Celts continued to dominate.

A week after the regular season concluded, Boston faced Syracuse again, the Nats having defeated the Warriors in the first round. The

Celtics had stayed sharp in the interim by scrimmaging against the New York Tuck Tapers of the Industrial League.

Dolph Schayes once again led the Nationals, with exciting new scorers Hal Greer and Dick Barnett complementing tough veterans such as Red Kerr and Larry Costello. Despite all the stars in their firmament, they had posted a losing season during the regular season. Still, after two games in the playoffs, they had managed to steal a win over Boston.

Bad feelings began boiling in the third game, a Celtics rout where Sharman scored 30 points while Russell scored 18, pulled down 39 boards, and blocked a bunch of shots. With a little more than four minutes remaining in the fourth quarter, Russ took an elbow in the eye from the Nats' 7'3" reserve center, Swede Halbrook, and collapsed to the court. Russell did not move for more than two minutes and then sat out the remaining time after he regained consciousness and staggered to the bench.

With the Celts up by one game, the teams traveled to Syracuse for the fourth, ferocious game. No one liked playing in the old Onondaga County War Memorial, and then as now, the city of Syracuse has rabid fans, no more so than this day. One Syracusan spent the entire first quarter throwing junk at Auerbach and jeering him.

In the second quarter Red called a timeout to get a clarification on a Mendy Rudolph call and then returned to the bench only to be shoved by the heckler. So Auerbach went after his tormentor, and when a second fan entered the fray, Jim Loscutoff threw him backward on his ass. Eventually, other Celtics and some Syracuse policemen restored order, as the Celtics won the fourth game handily. In the fifth game, back at the Garden, Boston clinched another trip to the Finals 123–101, again led by Sharman's scoring.

Once again, Boston faced the St. Louis Hawks, now almost totally dependent on the monster scoring of Bob Pettit and Cliff Hagan, squandering the talents of Lenny Wilkens and others. The Celtics won the series and another championship in five games. Fittingly, Bill Sharman had another terrific series, and although his defense had declined, he still had his shot until the end. The great guard had played way too many basketball games on those legs, not to mention baseball games and every other sport he indulged in. People do not appreciate the greatness of Bill Sharman or never knew much about him, a huge historical oversight that cannot be corrected enough.

Only recently, consumers gained the chance to purchase a banner containing all of the Celtics logos, including not only Lucky the Leprechaun but a figure from "circa 1960" that looks like Jack of "Jack Be Nimble" fame with a crown on his head jumping over a candlestick. "Jack" shows up on some Celtics programs or yearbooks of this era, and it is thought he is the creation of Les Stout, though little else is known about him. New England Patriots fans are split over the traditional Pat Patriot or the Flying Elvis logo, but no Celtics fan has yet been unearthed who prefers Jack over Lucky.

The NBA honored Bill Russell as its MVP, though he finished second at center to Wilt Chamberlain in the All-NBA voting. Like trying to accept time as having no beginning or end, it serves no useful purpose trying to fathom this concept. It just is.

After the season, the Celtics lost Gene Conley in the expansion draft to the Chicago Packers, an unappreciated loss, because he was a talented athlete and had spelled Russell when Bill took his rare breathers and had absorbed much punishment at forward. Had he played for the Celtics after his rookie year and not taken his sabbatical to dedicate himself to baseball, he might have provided the muscle down low to propel Boston into a championship series or two in those years before Russell.

Ill feelings between Bill Sharman and Walter Brown dominated much of the ensuing summer and fall. On one hand Brown stated that he wanted to Sharman to play two more years for him, but word also leaked out that if Sharman had returned, the Celtics had intended to expose him to the expansion draft for the new Chicago franchise. Ultimately, the Celtics decided that if they lost Sharman, they were losing him only to coach the new L.A. Jets team of the ABL, not to play for them also. On Boston's behalf, Bill Mokray pleaded, "Mr. Brown has an investment in

Sharman," while Brown himself huffed, "After all, I didn't quit on him. He quit on me."

Squeezing Sharman, NBA commissioner Maurice Podoloff accused him of trying "to induce other NBA players to break their contracts," while overseeing the league withholding Bill's playoff winnings of $3,400. A published cartoon of the time shows "ballplayers" Brown (No. 1) and Podoloff (No. 3400) trapping poor Sharman on the floor. Brown and the league wisely backed down, because had they invoked the reserve clause, it might not have worked, thereby opening up free agency.

The ABL challenge never materialized, as L.A. grounded the Jets in January, whereupon Bill became coach of the Cleveland Pipers, with a young George Steinbrenner as his boss. In that role, Sharman tentatively tried to wrest John Havlicek away from Boston. Most unforgiveable from a Celtics standpoint, he later coached the Lakers, leading them to a 33-game winning streak and later acting as their general manager. For his part, the classy Sharman has uttered only praise concerning Walter Brown.

chapter 13

We Love You, Cooz!

1961–62

Until now, it really had not been much of a rivalry. When the Lakers had played in Minnesota when George Mikan was leading that franchise to multiple championships, Boston had no one to challenge the great center and in fact had never advanced to play his team in the Finals. After Mikan left and Bill Russell came to Boston, the situation flipped, and even though the Lakers with Elgin Baylor played the Celtics for the championship in 1959, they had not defeated Boston in two years and then got swept in the Finals.

The next season, the last one the Lakers spent in Minnesota, they hit their nadir, rolling off a 25–50 record. But by 1961–62, Jerry West had joined Baylor, they had a decent coach in Fred Schaus and a couple of other good additions in Frank Selvy and Rudy Lo Russo, and they finished first in the Western Division.

Between seasons, the Celtics picked up swingman Carl Braun off waivers from New York; a five-time All-Star in the 1950s, he had run the course before he got to Boston and had rarely played. Red Auerbach gave two rookies a chance, guards Gary Phillips and Al Butler, but they did not stick either. Butler confounded; he played only a handful of games for the Celtics before Boston sold him to the Knicks, where he played three very solid years for them, scoring 600 to 800 points a year.

Suspended for three games, Red Auerbach had to temporarily turn the team over to player/coach Bob Cousy, who then ran up a perfect record.

Bill Russell won his second straight MVP Award, again playing about 1,000 more minutes than his nearest teammate and scoring 1,436 points, the highest in his career. Russell primarily defended, blocked shots, grabbed rebounds, and sparked the fast break, but in this first season without Bill Sharman, he helped more in the scoring.

Tommy Heinsohn also scored the most points in his career (1,742) as he joined Russell, Bob Cousy, and Sam Jones on the All-Star team. Guard K.C. Jones, for his part, had become one of the finest defenders at his position in the NBA, as did Satch Sanders (who more than doubled his minutes played over his rookie campaign) at forward.

The regular season did not present them with many challenges—the Celts went 60–20 after all—but the playoffs better resembled a run for Lord Stanley's Cup than a non-contact sport road to a championship. Against Wilt Chamberlain and the Warriors, the first round of the play-offs distilled into a win at home/lose away series with the teams tied after four games.

At the Garden, Game 5 devolved into a most violent game of musical chairs. It all started late in the game when Sam Jones drove to the basket and Wilt clotheslined him. They verbally jousted, and then Sam ran off the court to grab a stool, with which to either tame Wilt or at least keep him at bay. In the immortal words of sportswriter Clif Keane, "It was then that Wilt looked like a lion, after having impersonated a lamb on the court all afternoon." Russell tried to break it up as the benches emptied and Chamberlain started chasing Jones all over the court.

Jim Loscutoff went after the Warriors' Guy Rodgers and leveled him, after which Rodgers ran away from him, eventually grabbing and brandishing the stool for his own self-protection.

Somewhere along the line, Rodgers found time to punch Boston's Carl Braun. Rodgers ran away, as was his custom, smack into a gaggle of Celtics fans, who started taking their own shots at Rodgers.

When play resumed, Heinsohn got ejected after charging a Warrior lesser light, a miscarriage of street justice because another Warrior, Tom Meschery, had committed his sixth and final foul by practically mugging Tommy earlier.

Cousy and Warrior veteran Paul Arizin watched the whole circus without participating in it. As Cooz explained after the game, "We always pair off on things like that. We stand there and do nothing because we're both too old for fighting."

Bottom line, the Celtics won, with Russell scoring only one fewer point than Wilt while snaring more than double the rebounds Wilt pulled down.

Philly led basically the whole way to win the sixth game, setting up Game 7 back at the Garden. Often criticized for a lack of clutch play— or, more accurately, an unwillingness to take charge in such a situation— Sam Jones sank a 15-foot fadeaway shot to give the Celtics a 109–107 lead with two seconds remaining. Ed Conlin inbounded from midcourt, a pass to Chamberlain under the basket; but as proved so often the case, Russell swatted it away to preserve the victory, setting up a trip to the NBA Finals against the Lakers.

Tactically, Red Auerbach may have conceded that Elgin Baylor and Jerry West were going to post monster scoring numbers each night, or, equally true, he may not have had any choice in the matter. As expected, Baylor and West, with an assist from the largely forgotten Rudy LaRusso, carried L.A.'s offense, with Baylor scoring 61 points at the Garden in Game 5, giving the Lakers a 3–2 lead in the series.

Returning to Los Angeles, the Lakers seemingly had the series won at the half, leading by eight, but Boston overran them in the third, outscoring them by 18 points. Sam Jones led all scorers but it was the imbalance in the scoring distribution that doomed the Lakers. Boston had six scorers in double figures and Los Angeles only had three, as Boston coasted 119–105 to force a seventh and deciding game in the Garden.

In that fierce contest, the teams had stalemated late in regulation. Score tied 100–100. With 15 seconds left, Red had drawn up a play where Frank Ramsey would run off a screen from Russell and shoot the game winner. Except Rudy LaRusso floored Ramsey and did not get called for the foul. The Lakers regained possession with six seconds left, and Frank Selvy managed to find himself on the baseline, undefended, with the ball and the opportunity to bring the first championship to Los

Angeles. On a shot he never missed, he missed, sending the game into overtime.

Boston had survived, barely, with forwards Heinsohn, Loscutoff, and Sanders having all fouled out. It was Baylor's game to win, particularly because Elgin drew Ramsey to his sixth foul. The Celtics were down to Russell and three guards—Cousy, K.C. Jones, and Sam Jones—and off the bench, the seldom-used Gene Guarilia.

Inexplicably, in one of those transcendent moments, somehow Gene Guarilia owned the great Elgin Baylor in the remainder of OT. Maybe it was because his legs were rested, but Guarilia earned his less-than-15-minutes of fame that day, defending and rebounding well and causing Baylor to take poor shots, two of which he partially deflected. Behind Guarilia, Boston outscored the Lakers and held on to a 110–107 lead as Cousy dribbled the ball away from all defenders, just like the old days at the Boston Arena.

Boston had just won its fifth championship.

It was not all Guarilia, of course; he got some help from Bill Russell with 40 rebounds and 30 points, 23 key points from Ramsey off the bench, and 27 points by Sam Jones, almost all in the second half. Baylor and West carried their team, scoring a total of 76 points, almost enough.

Red lit another cigar.

1962–63

Everybody wanted this guy. Bill Sharman and George Steinbrenner of the ABL Cleveland Pipers sought him, as did the Cleveland Browns, drafting this big super-athlete as a potential tight end in the seventh round (out of 20 rounds) in the 1962 NFL draft. Red Auerbach did not care—he picked John Havlicek in the first round of the NBA draft because he calculated that if he signed the swing man from Ohio State, his Celtics teams would continue to dominate in the 1960s and possibly beyond.

It was not a sure thing. Havlicek posted faster times than anyone on the Cleveland Browns except for Bobby Mitchell, extending his tryout with the team until the last cut, when his football career ended. Not shabby for someone who had not played football since high school. Red

An astute Celtics observer can almost always tell from John Havlicek's hair what era a photo of Hondo was taken. This photo was undoubtedly taken in the 1970s, judging from his long locks—and the absence of fans in the upper decks of the Garden.

Auerbach then brought his rookie into camp and verified what he had heard, never having seen him play before the draft: "[Havlicek's] going to be a great one. Some days he reminds me of Ramsey, since he can play the backcourt or the front line. Other days he reminds me of [Tom] Gola—good 'ball-stealing' hands and fine anticipation."

In no way does it diminish the accomplishments of Hall of Famers Ramsey and Gola to suggest that for once, Red had grossly understated his point.

Havlicek grew up in Ohio with Phil and Joe Niekro, playing in abandoned strip mines. Like Bill Sharman and Sam Jones, he excelled in every sport he tried, an all-state football, basketball, and baseball player, though he displayed none of the intemperance or stubbornness of Sharman. Overlooked on a 1960 NCAA national championship team with Jerry Lucas and Bobby Knight, he made the United States Olympic team only as an alternate.

Instead of gasping and declining by the mid-1960s, the Boston Celtics thrived with their new sixth man, a strong defender as well as a shooter and a playmaker.

Jack Foley, a second-round draft choice who represented the last generation of Holy Cross Crusaders on the Celtics, played for them briefly before Auerbach sold him to the Knicks. Much more important, the club picked up center Clyde Lovellette, a future Hall of Famer who still had a couple years left, hoping he might contribute the minutes off the bench missed so dearly since Gene Conley had left.

The advent of the long career of Havlicek coincided with the swan song of Bob Cousy, in his final year as a player, having already accepted a job coaching the Boston College basketball team after his retirement, confessing, "I didn't tire of the game of basketball itself. I got tired of 50,000 miles of traveling a year, sick of suitcases and cab drivers and restaurants, tired of being away from Missie and the kids. I wanted to try coaching, and when Boston College asked me, I said yes."

When Cousy came to the Celtics, along with him came a tradition of making the playoffs each year. He had led the NBA in assists on eight occasions, and even in his final season he finished third in that category. Voted the NBA's Most Valuable Player in 1957, he participated in the All-Star Game every year that he played, voted the MVP in two of those exhibitions. He defended well and often ended up in the top 10 for scoring.

That merely scratches the surface, of course; he meant so much to the team and the region, helping to bring a national championship to Holy Cross and then deciding to settle in Worcester, officially becoming one of us. He facilitated the fast break and made everyone on his team better— or at least appear to be. He spoke out on issues and then walked the walk by befriending Chuck Cooper and easing his way into professional basketball in a still segregated America, in a land where racial slurs were commonplace put-downs. He served as a point guard before the position

The Celtics did not honor their stars adequately until Bob Cousy retired. Since then, the franchise has become increasingly adept at staging events for their departing luminaries.

had been dubbed as such, patiently but thrillingly leading his team down the court with impossible dribbling. He excelled before the 24-second shot clock and exploited it afterward.

On March 17, 1963, the fans of the Garden celebrated Bob Cousy Day as the Celtics took on the Syracuse Nationals, a team that gave the Cooz fits as a player but like him had reached its last regular season game ever. They would move to Philadelphia the next year to become the 76ers, but they still had one last game to play.

Cousy attempted to read his thanks to the crowd, often faltering due to emotion. At one point a fan bellowed out, "We love you, Cooz!" It broke the tension and permitted Cousy to continue his speech, a tear-jerker for the ages. Though the great guard scored only eight points that day, it put him over 1,000 for the season, something he had always done.

The man who bellowed out his, and Celtic Nation's, appreciation for Bob Cousy earned the temporary moniker as "The Voice." The Voice actually was Southie's Joe Dillon, who was then given free tickets to the playoffs for his display of fanaticism.

But Cousy and the team still had the playoffs ahead, facing Oscar Robertson and the Cincinnati Royals in their opening round. By now the best guard in basketball, Robertson had the support of Hall of Famer Jack Twyman at forward, along with Wayne Embry at center and Bob Boozer at the other forward position. Had Jerry Lucas played with them that year, they might have won the championship.

Fortunately, Boston still had Cousy and more important, Bill Russell. Tommy Heinsohn continued to demonstrate his excellence in the playoffs, a scorer who somehow found even more shots at season's end, this from a man who never pursued anything resembling an iron man fitness regimen. In the seventh game, Oscar Robertson scored 43 points, but Sam Jones answered with 47, and the Celtics advanced to the Finals.

It was an odd series. Though most of the games against the Lakers were close, Boston took it in L.A. in six games. Jerry West and Elgin Baylor accounted for way too much of their team's scoring, while Boston, in the sixth game for instance, had six of its eight players on the floor score in double digits, including Cousy with 18.

Bill Russell was named the MVP again this season, while John Havlicek earned recognition as a first-team rookie, though Terry Dischinger won Rookie of the Year. An All-Star his first three years in the NBA, Dischinger then served his country in the army for two years, but after he returned, he never regained his star status, even though he remained an accurate shooter. The Naismith Memorial Basketball Hall of Fame in Springfield, Massachusetts, is large enough for an exhibit for players like Dischinger, who sacrificed their careers to serve in the armed services.

chapter 14

Red's Last Stand and Russell's First

1963–64

K.C. Jones had the unenviable task of replacing Bob Cousy as a starter, but Red Auerbach had already carved out his role, recognizing in Jones' rookie season that he had "an All-American who couldn't shoot." Auerbach counseled Jones on his role, and in turn K.C. observed Cousy and worked on ways to replicate parts of Cooz's game, particularly controlling the tempo of the game, playing tight defense, and distributing the ball wisely. Said Auerbach, "From the day he reported, he did everything I asked him. He went in and dogged his man, whether it was for 30 seconds or 30 minutes." For the next three years, he specialized in defense and playmaking.

Jones had roomed with Bill Russell at the University of San Francisco and famously uttered only a handful of words to his roommate each day, until he finally opened up, a shock to Bill when it finally occurred. No longer bashful as a Celtic, Jones kept the team loose by imitating Cooz's gait and Russell's penetrating stare. This talent served him well as a player and then later during his tenure as the Celtics coach. Unfortunately for K.C., between his two-year hitch in the service and his apprenticeship waiting for Cousy to retire, by the fall of 1963, he was already 31 years old.

Foreseeing the inevitable, Auerbach had signed a former teammate of John Havlicek's, Larry Siegfried, to a free agent contract. What a terrific pickup! The Cincinnati Royals had chosen Siggy third overall in the 1961

One of the more reserved players in Celtics history, K.C. Jones' calm demeanor proved a perfect antidote to the methods of Celtics coach Bill Fitch years later, as Jones took over the helm and guided a veteran team to two NBA titles.

draft, but because the University of Cincinnati had just denied Ohio State its second national championship in the NCAA tournament, along with some incidents between the schools, he refused to sign with the Royals. Instead he played with the short-lived Cleveland Pipers and then taught high school. Astutely, Auerbach met the young schoolteacher in the locker room during a Celtics game and asked him to sign, thus picking up a tough player who knew the game, shot accurately, handled the ball well, and defended tenaciously for the waiver price of $1,000. A steal.

It was lucky that free agent Larry Siegfried succeeded, for Boston whiffed on all of its draft selections this year, with not one of them playing a second in the NBA. The most curious case involves Bill Green of Colorado State, the Celtics' first selection and ninth overall pick and a young man with a deathly fear of flying. Some particularly rough trips in college only heightened his terror, as he later described it: "One time we were on our way back from Utah and the plane was definitely out of control. Baggage was falling out at the back of the plane. People had started praying. Everyone was panicked. I decided it was time to be concerned. Then I got stuck in a rainstorm over Mississippi. After that, I just couldn't deal with it." Red tried to wheedle and cajole him all during camp and the preseason exhibitions, permitting him to take trains, but had to cut him as he never could overcome his phobia. Had Green suited up for Boston, the string of uninterrupted championships might have extended well into the 1970s. Green's story has an uplifting end. He became an educator, the principal of the troubled Jordan Mott School in the South Bronx, and was responsible for turning the program around, beloved and respected by his students and their parents. But he never flew again.

During the season, Oscar Robertson and the Cincinnati Royals won their series against Boston, frankly dominating the Celtics at times, but in the playoffs their star forward Jerry Lucas labored under a cranky back. Plus, during the season, the club had traded Bob Boozer for Larry Staverman, an awful swap, so Cincy simply did not have enough good players to assist Robertson. Sensing this, Auerbach plastered K.C. Jones against Oscar every game, with Jones admitting, "I don't like to play a man like that—all over the court when he doesn't have the ball. It's like cheating. It isn't fair to him."

Frank Ramsey trumped Red Auerbach as the most controversial Celtic this year, having participated in the preparation of an article in *Sports Illustrated* concerning how to draw fouls. The sainted among us chastised Ramsey for detailing this skill, complete with artist's accompanying sketches, as pure unsportsmanlike conduct. Most of it was misdirected envy by the critics, but Ramsey's game necessarily had to rely on guile and finding every edge, as age had robbed him of his ability to surge into a game and produce results immediately. At the breakup dinner that year, the Kentucky Colonel, Frank Ramsey, announced his retirement, despite Auerbach's entreaties to stay. Ramsey's post-playing career biography is not one of descent and despondency, as he became a full-time banker and made millions, much more than he made in the NBA.

Fair or unfair, the Celtics won their first round of the playoffs in five games and then trounced Wilt Chamberlain and the San Francisco Warriors in the Finals.

Bill Russell, Tommy Heinsohn, and K.C. Jones accompanied Red Auerbach and a host of other NBA All-Stars on a State Department goodwill tour of Eastern Europe. Well behind the Iron Curtain, in Kraków, Poland, Heinsohn heard an ominous knock on the door. He opened it to find two KGB stooges who told him to "grab your passport and come with us," apparently for questioning or brainwashing, as the case might be. Heinsohn was scared out of his mind, as he was whisked out to some communist version of a gin joint. The two agents told him to sit there as they disappeared into the darkness, the way one would expect spies to act. Heinsohn ran out of the building, almost directly into the outstretched cigar of Red Auerbach. Auerbach had asked two of the Polish coaches to pull the prank on Heinsohn, and they seemingly played their parts too well. Believing that revenge is a dish best served cold, Heinsohn patiently waited for the right moment to strike, and as soon as Red had begun to let down his guard, he lit up one of his stogies, only to have it blow up in his face.

1964–65

*"Havlicek steals it. Over to Sam Jones. Havlicek stole the ball! It's all over!
Johnny Havlicek is being mobbed by the fans!"*

John Havlicek and Celtics broadcaster Johnny Most instantly achieved immortality with that one play, one of the most famous stolen balls in franchise history, as Boston narrowly defeated the 76ers to advance to the NBA Finals against the Lakers.

A rare mental error preceded the epic play, as Bill Russell hit a wire inbounding the ball, relinquishing possession to the Sixers.

Against L.A., Boston dominated, winning another championship in five games. Tommy Heinsohn maintained his prowess in the playoffs, when injuries did not sideline him. The great forward had the off-season to ponder returning to action or calling a premature end to his career, but everyone expected him back.

Tragically, on September 7, 1964, club owner Walter Brown died on Cape Cod after sustaining a massive coronary, the great man endowed with a big heart but not a strong one. Tributes flowed from the media and virtually every prominent sportsman, politician, or prince of the church; Boston's Cardinal Cushing celebrated his life at St. Ignatius Church in Chestnut Hill, lauding Brown at appropriate length. More succinctly, one of the local newspapermen dubbed him "Man's Best Friend." That year, Red Auerbach carried around a St. Christopher medal with him in honor of his owner and friend.

Auerbach and Lou Pieri assumed even more prominent roles until Pieria and Brown's widow, Marjorie, sold the club to the Ruppert Knickerbocker Brewing Company, a subsidiary of Melvin Kratter's National Equities. Within two years, Pieri too had died.

The warm, almost familial relationship between ownership and the players faded as a series of owners have followed, some good and some dreadful. Increasingly Red Auerbach became the heart and soul of the franchise, embodying the central pursuit of excellence established by

Brown as corporate interests and player agents profited from Brown's initial vision. Incapable of exemplifying Brown's underlying humility, Auerbach nonetheless endowed the franchise with his own brand of humanity, as know-it-alls who knew nothing about basketball increasingly encroached on the Celtics in upcoming seasons.

In October 1966, the Celtics retired Bill Sharman's number, a few years after Bob Cousy and Ed Macauley had their numbers retired. The delay might have occurred because Sharman had coaching duties that kept him away or because a couple of players wore his No. 21 during this period. Maybe, but it always seemed that Bill Sharman became a bit of a Celtics orphan after he left the team, not totally cut out but treated a bit coolly nonetheless.

1965–66

Tommy Heinsohn wasn't coming back after all. He almost announced his retirement at the Celtics' season-ending send-off fete but took the summer to consider his options. Instead, the time away from the parquet merely reinforced Heinsohn's outlook, as he walked in pain every day during his vacation. He was retiring and he would be missed.

And yet, Heinsohn's retirement paled in comparison to the announcement by Red Auerbach that after the 1965–66 season, he intended to step down as head coach, having endured too many 20-hour workdays. Red defiantly gave every franchise and its fans one more shot at him.

The Celtics bombed out again in the draft, choosing Ollie Brown with their first draft choice, a man who never played in the league. Later-round picks Toby Kimball and Ronnie Watts did contribute a bit, but the Brown choice hurt, with Heinsohn retiring and the club aging. Brown was chosen ahead of the Van Arsdale twins, Keith Erickson, Bob Weiss, John McGlocklin, and Bob Love.

Not to worry! The team picked up Don Nelson as a free agent, a forward who played every day and became an increasingly better shooter as his career progressed. A Hall of Famer due to his later incarnation as a coach, his addition was huge given the increasing age of the core players on the team.

They needed the help. Other teams had caught up with them in talent and in depth, with the Philadelphia 76ers besting them in their regular season series behind Wilt Chamberlain, Hal Greer, Billy Cunningham, Chet Walker, Wali Jones, and Luke Jackson. In this changing climate, Boston came in second in the Eastern Division, behind the Sixers, and went all five games in the first round of the playoffs before defeating the Cincinnati Royals. Red exhorted his team to win with his slogan, "Dollars and Defense."

Facing the Sixers in the Eastern Division Finals, the Celtics dispensed with their rivals in five games, a seemingly incongruous result unless one followed the career of Wilt Chamberlain. While flowers blossomed in the spring, Wilt wilted.

Just as surely, Boston faced the Lakers in the NBA Finals, a series stretching seven games, with the penultimate contest fittingly in the Garden for Red's last home game. With 16 seconds remaining in regulation and with the Celtics ahead by six points, Massachusetts governor John Volpe lit Red Auerbach's cigar, signifying victory as the fans swarmed the court.

The cigar had been lit too early. In basketball, 16 seconds is not an eternity, yet it often seems that way. After the Celtics players helped push the crowd back to the edges of the court, play resumed and Boston nearly literally handed the game over to L.A., with miscues cutting the lead to two points with six seconds remaining.

Had hubris finally caught up with Red Auerbach? Naaaah. K.C. Jones took the inbound pass, and despite almost disappearing in the midst of Lakers defenders, he passed off to Havlicek, who killed the clock and got Red his last championship as a coach.

For Arnold "Red" Auerbach, the stress of coaching a dynasty had ended. For their new coach, William Fenton Russell, the ride had just begun.

1966–67

This is the year that the dynasty died, at least temporarily. After stepping down as coach, Red Auerbach persuaded Bill Russell to become a player/coach, the best guarantee in keeping Russell as a player. Never having coached before, the transition was not always smooth, but the club still finished the season at 60–21, almost .200 points higher than the leading Western Division team. Unfortunately, this was the Philadelphia 76ers' year, as Wilt Chamberlain either temporarily decided to be unlike himself, or else he simply had too much talent surrounding him not to succeed. Coach Alex Hannum had seemingly mesmerized Wilt into becoming a team player nonpareil.

Not that Auerbach went quietly into the night—he traded backup center Mel Counts to the Baltimore Bullets straight up for forward Bailey Howell, a one-sided trade for Boston as Howell scored nearly 5,000 points in the next four years. Shrewdly, Auerbach then replaced Counts with Wayne Embry, trading a third-round pick to the Royals.

Bailey Howell played with intensity, a very nice man who seemed to always finish somewhere in the top 10 league-wide in fouls committed. Getting up for each game was not easy, as he later described, "Because teams got the best crowds on weekends, we played a lot of back-to-back Friday night, Saturday night, and Sunday afternoon games. And if we were traveling, it meant you had to catch commercial flights. No team had private jets with food waiting to be served on board like today's teams do. You really had to be mentally tough. Everybody was tired. Sometimes, you couldn't catch a flight out after a Friday night game and you wouldn't walk into the arena for the Saturday night game until just before game time. Then you'd go to the next game site, get there at 4:00 in the morning on Sunday, and play at 2:00 in the afternoon."

Both transactions kept the Celtics competitive, particularly hard for a team that drafted late each round and then chose poorly after Havlicek's rookie year. Howell brought tools to the team, excelling in shooting, scoring, rebounding, and defending, exactly what you might expect from a six-time All-Star and future Hall of Famer. Belying his calm and folksy exterior, this guy banged bodies like a Big Bad Bruin, Gomer Pyle on steroids. Embry no longer possessed the rebounding or shooting skills that propelled him to five All-Star selections, but he towered over the departing Counts and played very effectively in his new role as Bill Russell's backup. Auerbach the GM wanted to provide Russell the coach with as many weapons as possible, but he also wanted to keep Russell the player healthy. Howell and Embry did that, moving bodies around and keeping their player/coach on the floor at a game's most critical moments.

K.C. Jones retired at season's end, and though fantasy leaguers will never comprehend what made Jones such a terrific player, perhaps Red Auerbach explained it most succinctly: "He really couldn't shoot that well or pass that well or do anything great. But every time I put him in the game, the score got bigger in our favor. When I took him out, we were always further ahead than when he went in."

In the playoffs, the Celtics cruised past the Knicks, squaring off against Philly in the Eastern Division Finals. Despite the 76ers' excellent 68–13 regular season record, Boston actually prevailed (by one game) in their regular season matchups. In their previous two games, Philly won the first by two points in overtime, while Boston won the next, three days later, by two points. That was then.

The Sixers' Alex Hannum was a good coach and a funny man. Asked why he had statistically lost an inch since his playing days had ended, he replied, "I got bald." Later, when he coached in the ABA, he opined that the red-white-and-blue basketball belonged only on the end of a seal's nose.

The Sixers dominated the series, winning in five. Alex Hannum outsmarted Russell the coach while Wilt outplayed Russell the center. Onlookers saw Hal Greer breezing past K.C. Jones and Satch Sanders not playing his usual peerless defense. Poor Bailey Howell had to endure the horror of having to worry about his daughter, seriously injured while falling out of the second-story window of their home in West

Roxbury. In the final game of their series, Philadelphia blew Boston out 140–116.

The dynasty was over; the king had died. Long live Wilt.

Or so they thought. One problem—the king had not died. While Wilt spent the off-season farting around deciding whether to buy a team, fight Muhammad Ali, or play for the New York Jets, Bill Russell was getting even. Surrounded by unlit cigars, general manager Red Auerbach was getting mad.

chapter 15

All Things Must Pass

1967–68

Before Boston rebuilt, it had to lose its youth, as the Supersonics chose Ron Watts and the Rockets chose Jim Barnett and Toby Kimball in the NBA expansion draft in May. Gambling that his veterans still had enough stamina and talent to compete, Red Auerbach did not expose them to the draft. An old team had just gotten older.

In many ways, this year revolved around the growth of Don Nelson. Stylistically, Bill Russell had decided to delegate a lot of decision making on the court to trusted veterans such as Sam Jones and John Havlicek, asking them to assume these added roles before the season began. As a future Hall of Fame coach, Nelson thrived in this type of system where his court smarts exceeded almost every opponent he faced. He played more minutes and developed a feared scoring touch, as he finished the season in the top 10 in scoring percentage for the first time.

Increasingly though, this was John Havlicek's team, as Hondo, no longer considered a sixth man, led the team in scoring and minutes played while defending well, racing up and down the court breathlessly. Sam Jones had his last great scoring season, while Bill Russell continued his defensive brilliance. Despite their determination to avenge the results of the previous year, the Celtics finished eight games behind the Eastern Division–winning Philadelphia 76ers.

On April 4, 1968, Martin Luther King Jr. was assassinated in Memphis, Tennessee, precipitating Boston and Philadelphia postponing a playoff game "out of deference to the national day of mourning" for Dr. King. Bill Russell predicted a collision between the races. He was right. Facing a 40–42 Detroit Pistons in the Eastern Division semis, Boston fell behind after losing the second and third games. It is a largely forgotten series now, but Pistons guard Dave Bing scored virtually at will, and he received a lot of support from Dave DeBusschere, Happy Hairston, Eddie Miles, Terry Dischinger, and Jimmy Walker (Jalen Rose's father). Unfortunately, their centers, Jim Fox and former Celtics draftee Joe Strawder, could not contain Bill Russell offensively or defensively.

The Pistons, correctly discerning their need for a center, thereafter traded DeBusschere to New York for Walt Bellamy and Howie Komives and promptly fell completely apart.

Now it was Boston's turn to crumble against the Sixers in the Eastern Division Finals, as the team lost two games at the Garden, poised for elimination after only four contests. The obituary writers typed away about the demise of Russell, and Red Auerbach mused, "There are some people who have already forgotten how great that man really was."

Russell refreshed their memories, as Sam Jones scored 37 and Havlicek 29, in a blowout of the Sixers in Philly. Despite Hal Greer's 40 points back at the Garden, Boston led most of the way for the win to tie the series. Back at the Spectrum, the rivals played a desperate game, as both Sam Jones and Bailey Howell fouled out, but Boston held on to win the series with a 100–96 victory. Defensively, Boston kept Greer and Chamberlain from killing them, and Boston had one element not present in the Sixers lineup—a sixth player. Don Nelson steadily contributed, and in such a close series, his presence, rarely noted, made the difference.

Russell had grown as a coach, as he outsmarted Alex Hannum, who promptly walked the plank as the Sixers coach. The Celtics, not Wilt and everyone else, would play the Los Angeles Lakers in the NBA Finals.

Idle for seven days, the Lakers lost the first game of the series to Boston, squandering a 15-point lead. Jerry West played on a bad ankle but did not use his injury as an excuse, nor did the Celtics' Satch Sanders, also hurt. Bill Russell had spoken about trying to defend West and Elgin Baylor, but he knew that they could only be contained. Instead, as he had done earlier against the Pistons, Russell scored more than normal, something he had the potential to do his entire career. Like Detroit, L.A.

had a Celtics castoff at the pivot, Mel Counts, no match against Russell for an entire title series. Russell played his bench and let his other starters engage in a point-scoring contest against the Lakers.

Weldon Haire, the Celtics public address announcer, had lost the right all season to introduce his team before each game as the "World Champion Celtics." He regained that right after Boston dispatched the Lakers in L.A. after Game 6.

1968–69

Sam Jones announced that he was retiring at the conclusion of 1968–69 season, somewhat surprising because he had just led the team at 21.3 points per game and a seemingly carefree approach: "You get out there and sometimes you have it, passing, shooting—sometimes you don't. It's all split seconds, and I just don't worry about it." Boston would miss his stutter step before driving by defenders, his geometrically sound bank shots, and his chiding of opponents for missing shots, but the team and its fans still had one more year to appreciate this clutch player.

Red Auerbach used to tell a story about how Sam Jones chose basketball over football. As quarterback, Jones shined, but on the third down he got clobbered, thereby ending his football career the moment he hit the turf. Great story but untrue—Jones was a very talented quarterback who fortunately liked basketball a bit better than the other sports at which he excelled.

Jones' announcement underscored what everyone knew: this was an old team lucky to have won the title the previous year. As events unfolded, the 1968–69 edition finished fourth in the Eastern Division with a 48–34 record, having lost a majority of its games in the second half of the season. The Celtics lost six of their seven contests against the Knicks and four of six against the Lakers.

The production of Russell, Jones, and Howell had dropped significantly. Don Nelson and Larry Siegfried picked up their games, and the additions of guard Em Bryant and rookie Don Chaney helped, but no savior filled the street meters and walked into the Cambridge YMCA to announce himself to his new teammates.

By design or chance, the Celtics possessed one advantage—rest, a luxury that had never presented itself during their more productive years. Russell no longer played crazy minutes and Sam Jones had missed 12 games, so two of the old veterans still could call on some reserves of energy in the playoffs.

Plus, they got a bit lucky. The Celtics won the first round against the Sixers in five games, which sounds dominant, but Philly no longer had Wilt Chamberlain in the pivot, having traded him to the Lakers. In their only loss, Boston shot almost two dozen times more from the floor than Philly, and in the last game, the Celtics won only because Em Bryant came up huge at the end. Similarly, against the Knicks, Walt Frazier sustained a groin injury, so naturally Russell and his men pounded the paint while Sam Jones scored 29 and Havlicek 28 in their one-point, clinching victory in the sixth game. Again, Em Bryant put his team over with 19 points.

But luck gets a team only so far, and in the Finals, the Lakers stood poised to finally defeat the Celtics. L.A. not only had Elgin Baylor and Jerry West but also had obtained Wilt Chamberlain down low and had won the Western Division.

The teams split the first four games as West and Havlicek went on huge scoring runs each game. West continued his rampage with 39 to lead L.A. to a victory in the fifth game, but back in Boston, Don Nelson scored 25 points and Em Bryant again played beyond expectations as Boston squared the series to set up the deciding game in Los Angeles. Each team had won at home, and in anticipation of a title, Lakers owner Jack Kent Cooke filled the rafters with balloons, scheduled to fall at the appropriate crowning moment.

Fortunately for the Celtics, the Lakers had Wilt Chamberlain. Behind most of the game, Wilt sustained a dubious knee injury with 5:19 remaining in the fourth. Without him, the Lakers continued to close the gap with former Celtic Mel Counts having a career quarter, so naturally

Wilt asked back in. His coach, Butch van Breda Kolff, refused to let Wilt return, reasoning that he needed real players with heart who thrived in this type of pressure, not a guy who begged out with a phantom injury who then begged in when his team fought back.

And the Lakers had closed the gap, trailing 103–102 after putting together a 19–3 run. Coolly, Don Nelson took the ball and took a shot from near the foul line that clanged between the backboard and the back of the rim, bounced high in the air, and then returned through the net for an improbable field goal. Boston had broken its mini-slump and hung on for the two-point victory. Said Nellie in the winner's locker room, "What can I say? It was a lucky shot, the luckiest shot of my life."

Clueless Wilt Chamberlain groused in the clubhouse, well on his way to killing another one of his coaches (former Holy Cross Crusader and Boston Celtic Joe Mullaney would take over the head coach's job in L.A.), having sunk his own team in the clutch and squandered one of the greatest performances in NBA history, that by Jerry West. West had just won a car as the MVP of the playoffs, yet he appreciated the emptiness of the honor: "Every year it gets more difficult to sit here and talk about it."

Sam Jones departed a winner, and hopefully Bill Russell meant to return to try to earn yet another championship.

Having largely ignored the Celtics, this year the City of Boston broke with tradition and staged a parade through its streets for its returning heroes.

1969–70

After the latest championship, Bill Russell still had one more year on a very lucrative contract as player/coach for the Celtics, but he decided during the summer to retire. He had lost his sense of "involvement," his "urge to win," the thing that helped separate him from his peers, and he simply refused to embarrass himself by not pushing himself and his players every night. As usual, Sam Jones had the last word on the Russell retirement: "What would you do if Sam Jones retired?" The Celtics were in a bad way, no longer able to feed the opposition straight to Russell.

In the 1950s and through the 1970s, American children bought and studied any number of books on how to improve the finer points of their basketball skills. In announcing his retirement from the NBA in *Sports Illustrated*, Bill Russell best distilled the essence of a winner who understood the sport: "Let's talk about statistics. The important statistics in basketball are supposed to be points scored, rebounds, and assists. But nobody keeps statistics on other important things—the good fake you make that helps your teammate score; the bad pass you force the other team to make; the good long pass you make that sets up another pass that sets up another pass that leads to a score; the way you recognize when one of your teammates has a hot hand that night and you give up your own shot so he can take it. All of those things. Those were some of the things we excelled in that you won't find in the statistics. There was only one statistic that was important to us—won and lost."

Poor Hank Finkel tried to post up but was no Bill Russell, a fact not lost on Auerbach, who spouted, "Finkel is Finkel. He can shoot, but on defense it's something else. The moment a switch shows, well...." In that vein, Red spent all summer and some of the fall trying to persuade Bill Russell to return, to no avail, causing Auerbach to deadpan that his old center "is getting fatter and fatter, so that means our chances of having him back are getting thinner and thinner."

Hank Finkel received a totally bad rap in Boston, expected to replace Bill Russell. Absorbing a continuum of abuse all season at home, he planned to retire after his first year in Boston, but Red Auerbach and Tommy Heinsohn convinced High Henry to stay. Besides, they had plans to build their team around a rookie center named Dave Cowens.

Meanwhile, new coach Tom Heinsohn brought his own hands-on style to coaching as his team worked out at the Tobin Gym in Roxbury. Puzzled by some of the intricacies of the No. 6 play, Heinsohn demonstrated it himself, taking and swishing the ball with a perfect jumper. What made the demonstration so impressive was that he never once stopped smoking his cigarette the whole time, astounding rookies and veterans alike.

Auerbach still loved his new choice for a head coach, explaining while waiving a lit cigar, "It's like this: I always admired Tommy. When he was a kid, getting all that money, all that publicity, he still was smart and built up a successful insurance business. I liked that. He's showed me he has tenacity of purpose. He's sincere, he thinks, and he doesn't lie." As tangible proof, Tommy unplugged the record player in the locker room, substituting it with a projector and films of the last game for his charges to analyze.

Regardless, Auerbach persisted in trying to convince Russell to stay, with Heinsohn claiming that he only knew he had the job of coach about three days before the season started. The GM loved Heinsohn but cherished Russell.

Lacking any experience as a coach, Heinsohn brought considerable intensity to his job; plus, he knew how the franchise thrived. He knew the Celtic Way. The real problem was that he lacked Russell at center, with tidal waves of driving opponents funneled into poor High Henry Finkel. Bailey Howell lost some of his effectiveness, and Satch Sanders lost the last two months of the season to a knee injury. No records exist to suggest that Satch might have escaped injury if he had worn those kneepads that Auerbach had hid on him so many years prior.

Siegfried, though, experienced one of the more meaningful moments of the season around Thanksgiving, when he started fighting with the Sixers' Wali Jones and old Celtic Gene Conley emerged from the stands to break up the fisticuffs. Siegfried played well, if inconsistently, but did not get along with Heinsohn, while Em Bryant incurred a $100 fine and a half-game suspension for conduct unbecoming a Celtic, the first suspension of a Celtic ever. Philosophized Tommy, "Obviously, I wasn't popular with a couple of [the players]; that's for sure. But it wasn't my duty to be popular with them. It was their duty to please me."

Clearly, Tommy Heinsohn possessed a unique style: Auerbach screamed at refs, Russell took a more collaborative approach as a player/coach, but Tommy pretty much exuded any and every emotion he was experiencing at the time. During one game, he tried to kick something in disgust and instead his shoe flew off his foot and into the Garden stands. Entertaining, but could he coach?

Like Finkel, Heinsohn received much of the blame for the Celtics' 34–48 season, the first time that Boston had not made the playoffs since Sam Adams drank his first beer—or at least since Doggie Julian had paced the parquet. Had Bill Russell decided to return, Red probably would have fired Heinsohn, but in this season of scapegoats, Auerbach refused to panic. Instead, in the expansion draft after the dreary campaign had ended, he exposed a declining talent in Bailey Howell and cast off insubordinates Em Bryant and Larry Siegfried. Wisely, he gave Heinsohn the opportunity to win or lose with his own people.

And Heinsohn still had weapons at his disposal: John Havlicek scored 24.2 points per game, a completely misleading statistic as this unselfish player also finished seventh league-wide in assists per game, while also voted second-team all defense. Offensively, Don Nelson had his best year, scoring more than 1,000 points for the first time and taking on more minutes on the floor. At the 1969 spring draft, Auerbach had wisely listened to Bill Russell, who urged him to choose guard Jo Jo White from the University of Kansas; along with Lew Alcindor and Bob Dandridge, White made All-Rookie that year despite playing in only 60 games, arriving after he had served some of his Marine obligations. White furnished a certain elegance to the team, a finesse player with a pristine shot, alloyed with an iron man's disposition.

And yet this glass was still more than half empty, in a bridge year that threatened to branch into a chasm unless a big man emerged to fittingly succeed the great Bill Russell. Had Russell played another year, they might have slid into the postseason, but to vie for championships, the Celtics needed to find a new superstar in the pivot. Red Auerbach thought he had his man.

chapter 16

Undisputed Rookie of the Year

1970–71

Before Dave Cowens won the Rookie of the Year Award, leading the league in personal fouls and establishing himself as one of the NBA's leading rebounders, the red-headed rookie was selected as the MVP of the annual Maurice Stokes Game in August, scoring 32 points. Designed by Jack Twyman and Milton Kutsher to help defray the medical expenses of Stokes—the Royals great who had suffered a seizure and became permanently paralyzed after falling on his head against the Lakers in 1958—the game featured NBA stars coached this year by Red Auerbach and Dolph Schayes. Right out of college, Cowens dominated. He also participated in Harlem's Rucker Tournament, keeping himself in shape all summer, mainly on city blacktop surfaces.

Legend tells us that Red Auerbach scouted Cowens at a Florida State game and left in the middle, shaking his head and looking annoyed to disguise his captivation with this young man's talent. Because Boston had stunk the year before, it possessed the fourth draft choice, and Red had to hope the three teams before him did not discover what he knew; he potentially had the greatest big man in franchise history—besides Bill Russell—in his sights.

On draft day, March 23, 1970, in New York, the Pistons selected future Hall of Famer Bob Lanier, filling a need at the pivot perhaps even greater than the Celtics. Next, the Rockets chose Michigan forward Rudy Tomjanovich, a five-time All-Star for them and probably a Hall of Fame lock before Kermit Washington Picassoed his face. Third came the Hawks, formerly of St. Louis, now of Atlanta. Years prior the Hawks had passed on Bill Russell, obtaining Easy Ed Macauley and Cliff Hagan from Boston, but this time they had no deal in place with the Celtics and could have

Dave Cowens is one of only four players in NBA history to lead his team in points, rebounds, assists, steals, and blocks in a single season (1977–78). The others are LeBron James, Scottie Pippen, and Kevin Garnett.

ruined things by choosing Cowens to back up an aging Walt Bellamy. Instead, they chose the talented but troubled Pistol Pete Maravich. Boston had its man.

As expected, Auerbach had more tricks to play that evening. In the second round, he barely missed an opportunity to choose Calvin Murphy and Nate Archibald, but he did throw a seventh-round selection at North Carolina's Charlie Scott, thus beginning a years' long obsession with obtaining the talented swing man. Boston whiffed this time, at least temporarily, as Scott signed with Virginia of the ABA.

Mal Graham, a Celtic for two seasons in the late-1960s, scouted Dave Cowens and hundreds of other prospects, being particularly impressed by the red-headed center from Florida State. Tommy Heinsohn never saw Cowens play in college, but on Graham's recommendation Red Auerbach watched the recruit and selected him. Mal Graham's talents as a keen judge of NBA-level talent is perhaps exceeded only by his knowledge of the law in his later incarnation as a justice on the Massachusetts Court of Appeals.

Like Larry Bird a decade later, the 6'9" Cowens transformed the Celtics from a loser to a winner in one season. He made everyone better, as Jo Jo White and forward Steve Kuberski more than doubled their previous year's scoring totals while John Havlicek exceeded 2,000 points for the first time in his career. With an improving Don Chaney at guard and Don Nelson wherever needed, Boston had removed many of its seemingly intractable weaknesses.

Back to Chaney, a shooting guard who in his first two years as a professional had demonstrated an aversion to accurate shooting. In the classic mid-dynastic Celtics era, Red either would have cut him as a classic mistake or told him never to shoot unless he had an undefended layup.

Because the team no longer had the luxury of tossing a player or over-specializing, Boston stuck with him. Not only did he realize his considerable potential as a defender, but he also developed a shot. A hideous .319 shooter from the floor in his rookie season, in this campaign he raised his level to a much more palatable .454. Unafraid of making contact, he soon became a perennial NBA All-Defensive selection. Not typically considered patient men, Auerbach and Heinsohn cultivated Chaney, an intelligent ballplayer who became a very good one.

It wasn't just Chaney who showed improvement; point guard Hambone Williams dished out assists, and all of the bench players now had important roles to play when they entered the fray. Everyone thrived under this system, a fast-breaking team where even the center and forwards raced down the court. Enthusiastic fans even stopped booing Hank Finkel and embraced High Henry.

John Havlicek noticed it early: "I'm scoring more, partially because I'm playing more. But another reason is that our fast break is working. I'm getting the ball closer to the basket and getting better-percentage shots. Dave's responsible. He's getting the ball and throwing it out quickly."

Dave Cowens was not the sole selection from Florida State that year—the club also chose forward Willie Williams, whose ambition was to one day play for the Celtics. He did live his dream, albeit shortly, as the club waived him in midseason, picked up by Bob Cousy and the Royals. Also, Red Auerbach used picks to get rights to ABA-bound players, as he had not only drafted Charlie Scott but also Bob Croft and Mike Maloy. In a quirk of the time, Cowens had already signed with the NBA, as had Jo Jo White previously, and when Boston picked them it assumed the terms of the existing contracts from the league, all designed to thwart any poaching of talent by ABA clubs.

The new-look Celtics, for the first time ever, trained and bunked at Hellenic College. When the real games began, they lost their first three and then settled into a pattern where they traded wins and losses liberally—winning five in a row and then losing four straight, that type of pattern. The team did honor Sam Jones by publicly retiring his number, causing the great guard to recall, "We were a team, not a bunch of individuals. A family team—you know, our wives were close friends and things like that. It was 12 good years."

As soon as it appeared those days had ended, never to return, that threat ended on November 25, when the Celtics defeated the Portland Trail Blazers, the commencement of a 10-game winning streak. Even before this, Heinsohn crowed, "We're playing just like the Celtics of old." After the streak ended, oddly enough so too did the Celtics' chances of making the playoffs after their one-year hiatus, as they lost the majority of their remaining games.

Problem was, they could not beat some of the better teams in the league, such as the Bucks and the Knicks, and split their series against the Bullets. They did not advance to the playoffs, despite John Havlicek having what Tommy Heinsohn claimed was the single best season by a Celtic ever. On some nights, Cowens looked great; on others, Lew Alcindor and Willis Reed torched him.

Cowens held his ground, though. In one chippy game against Buffalo's Bob Kauffman, the Braves veteran threatened Dave thusly: "You do that once more and I'm going to punch you in the [expletive deleted] mouth." Replied Cowens, "Go ahead," as he slugged Kauffman in the face, allegedly knocking out some teeth. Buffalo Bob responded by belting Cowens and cutting his eye. Dave Cowens did not back down.

Had Satch Sanders not required knee surgery in October, this team might have participated in the postseason, as an almost identical roster with a healthier Satch accomplished the feat the next season. Or maybe the team needed to gel or Heinsohn needed another season of coaching experience. In any case, Boston had rebuilt, prepared to win more NBA titles very soon.

Or most likely, the commissioner should have arranged it so that the team with the third-best record in the Eastern Conference played in the playoffs. Due to systemic flaws, Boston (which finished both third in the Atlantic Division and the entire Eastern Conference) had to defer to the two top teams in the Eastern Conference's Central Division: the Bullets, who had barely scraped past .500, and the Hawks, who lost 10 more games than they won. The Celtics were penalized by their status as an Atlantic Division team.

Cowens missed a couple flights that year (once when his car died in the Callahan Tunnel on the way to Logan Airport), but by then Boston fans had fallen in love with him. When the Rookie of the Year Award went jointly to him and the Blazers' prolific scorer Geoff Petrie, his teammates were furious. They rightly felt that their red-haired center stood in a class of one. They were right—in a poll of NBA players taken by *The Sporting News*, Cowens' peers dubbed him Rookie of the Year by a 4–1 spread over Petrie.

People no longer spoke of bringing the great Russell back to Boston.

1971–72

Gypped out of the playoff the previous season by the league's divisional structure, the Celtics convincingly removed all controversy by outright winning the Atlantic Division. A nice mix of Auerbach-coached Celtics (Havlicek, Sanders, and Nelson) and star young players (Cowens, White, and Chaney) had restored the franchise.

This was a horrible time for the Celtics in the draft; they either lacked funds or financial commitment from ownership, so they deliberately passed on UCLA's Curtis Rowe, figuring that they could not sign him. Instead, they used the 10th overall pick on Clarence Glover, which did them no good. They drafted Dave Robisch in the third round, but he signed with the ABA's Denver Rockets and had a decent start of his career with them. In the end Glover scored only 65 points as a professional, while big man Robisch scored more than 10,000, playing for virtually everybody. Rowe made one NBA All-Star team; had he learned and personified the Celtics system as a rookie, he might be remembered today not as a pariah but rather as a stalwart on the talented teams of the early 1970s.

Larry Bird had his famous scrape at Chelsea's, and so too did Dave Cowens in his day down South, where a knife-wielding assailant stabbed the young Celtic in his right arm. Cowens was treated and released, and the whole incident simply faded into life's rich pageant.

Humbled the past two seasons, the new Celtics measured their progress by beating the new standards of excellence. They defeated Milwaukee 125–114 early in the season, but still the "Knicks jinx" kept confounding them. Having lost eight straight to New York, the challenge to reverse the curse loomed leading up to the Celtics' December 7 game with their rivals. Muscle spasms in his lower back victimized Dave Cowens, jeopardizing his ability to participate in this critical game.

These were Red Holzman's Knickerbockers: Willis Reed and Jerry Lucas at center; Bill Bradley and Dave DeBusschere at forward; and Walt Frazier, Earl Monroe, and Dick Barnett at guard. So Holzman had six future Hall of Famers and a good bench to call on, a pretty formidable congregation. Against them the Celtics called on only two future Hall of Famers, Cowens and Havlicek (Satch Sanders made it as a contributor, and Jo Jo White deserves induction). Tommy Heinsohn, though, saw some flaws in this team, fissures that ultimately unglued this opposing upcoming dynasty: they were age and injury. Indeed, Willis Reed missed almost the entire regular season. Confidently, Heinsohn predicted his Celtics would win the Atlantic Division, which meant that they had to start beating New York.

On December 7, at Madison Square Garden, the Knicks jinx fell 105–97. Walt Frazier scored 25 points, but so did Hondo, and Jo Jo White topped everyone with 26. Cowens played only 16 minutes but pulled down 11 rebounds, and Satch Sanders neutralized Dave DeBusschere. In the third, the Celtics' fast break decimated New York, as they outscored the Knicks 31–14. Jinx over, although not every Celtic prospered, as rejuvenated play by Sanders curtailed the playing time of young forward Steve Kuberski.

By way of a brief diversion, as Christmas approached, some of the players' families visited the wives' homes as the team spent the holiday playing in Cincinnati, but for others remaining in Massachusetts, they spent Christmas morning at Satch Sanders' home. So when you hear that back in the day the Celtics were like a family, they were.

The Celtics' resurgence did not change one basic fact—Boston still stumbled against one excellent team, defeating Los Angeles only once during the regular season. Then again, most teams paled when compared to the 69–13 Lakers under their new coach, Bill Sharman. Similar to Billy Martin in baseball, Sharman possessed the keen ability to produce dramatically positive results almost immediately, and in his first year at the helm, he even had notoriously work-skeptical Wilt Chamberlain buying into his then-revolutionary insistence on game day shootarounds. With Wilt keyed into the team concept, at least momentarily, Sharman rolled over his opponents with a roster peopled with other stars such as Gail Goodrich, Happy Hairston, Jerry West, and an ailing Elgin Baylor. He even had a defensive specialist at forward, à la Satch Sanders, in Keith Erickson. The championship passed through Los Angeles this year.

As predicted, the Celtics won the Atlantic Division, eight games ahead of New York and 26 games in front of a 76ers team that collapsed (the next season they turned in their historic 9–73 record). Commencing the playoffs, the Celtics squared off against Atlanta, the Hawks sporting a poor regular season 36–46 performance. Heinsohn figured out early that the series had devolved into a shootout, so his team went all out to take the series in six, for the privilege of facing the Knicks in the Eastern Conference Finals. Offensively, Havlicek played out of his mind.

The thinking was that after they dispatched the Knicks, who had lost Reed for the duration, the Celtics would meet their West Coast nemesis, the Los Angeles Lakers, for the NBA title.

Boston never got there.

In the first matchup at the Boston Garden, the Knicks blew the Celtics away, though the *Boston Globe's* Bob Ryan did allow that Boston "stayed in the game until the center jump which began the first period." Bill Bradley and Dave DeBusschere swarmed Hondo and Cowens. Quite uncharacteristically, Don Nelson gave up the ball like he was donating it to charity. Then the Knicks defeated Boston by one point when the series moved to Madison Square Garden. Frazier seemingly divined his shots into the net, even though he played only half of this second game.

The Celtics redeemed themselves, winning the third game as Cowens returned from the recently departed and Hondo took over the fourth period, grabbing rebounds and scoring in the clutch along with Jo Jo White.

Then they became unglued. The defining term of the series, *poise*, eluded Boston, to the monopolization of the Knicks. In Game 4, White and Havlicek, despite their valiant efforts, failed to keep Boston alive as Cowens again fell short. And then the fights started. Kuberski and Rex Morgan fought, respectively, the Knicks' Luther Rackley and Charley Paulk. Rackley, so enraged at Kuberski, charged into the Celtics locker room after the game to take off Steve's head, restrained by his teammate Willis Reed, who restored order. Boston now trailed 3–1.

Havlicek, Nelson, and White tried, but DeBusschere and the Knicks won the fifth and fatal game at Boston Garden, and just like that, the season ended. Satch Sanders did not neutralize the opposing scorers, and Dave Cowens too often scored way too little, leaving most of the offensive chores to his teammates. Conversely, New York possessed too many weapons and a deeper bench (Heinsohn may not have known the names of three of his own reserves), and they had more veterans who had been there before.

So now all of the Celtics had been there.

chapter 17

To Be Champions Once Again

1972–73

This was the great Celtics championship season that never was. Similar to the Lakers from a season ago, the Celtics rarely lost, posting a 68–14 record as young players such as Dave Cowens and Jo Jo White became team legends.

One thing that the Knicks taught Red Auerbach and Tommy Heinsohn that stuck was that Cowens, with all of his talent and desire, needed more help up front.

Augmenting an already improving club, Auerbach traded the rights to Charlie Scott to the Phoenix Suns for Paul Silas, an astonishing addition. For basketball lovers of a certain bent, Paul Silas represents everything a Celtics fan wants out of a player; he was tough, smart, unselfish, and dedicated to pursuing team goals, someone who never looked faintly lost on the basketball court in his career. Even though he did not play center, had he suited up for the pre–Bill Russell Celtics in the 1950s, he would have protected Ed Macauley and those Celtics would have won rings.

The previous season, Silas had scored more than 17.5 points per game, a career best, but Red and Heinsohn saw something different, an ability and a drive that once channeled made both the player and his new team considerably better. With a short center that often played like a forward, the club wanted someone tough to have Cowens' back and pull down rebounds. Silas still scored points, but he subordinated that aspect of his repertoire to become a leading offensive and defensive rebounder.

By embracing and understanding his role, Silas had the potential to vault his team deep into the playoffs, and to his credit, he did.

Not that he came easy. Essentially Suns GM Jerry Colangelo had jumped the gun by signing Charlie Scott, who had played most of the year with the Virginia Squires, late in the 1971–72 season. Because Boston still retained its draft rights to Scott, Colangelo had to negotiate a trade, and Red held his guns to demanding Silas in return. Colangelo wanted both Scott and Silas and spent much of the summer of 1972 trying to have it both ways. The gambit failed, and after Silas came to terms with Boston, Howie McHugh picked him up at the airport and initiated the process of transforming Silas into a born-again Celtic.

It worked, for after he arrived at Logan Airport as a certified Doubting Thomas concerning the Celtics mystique, he quickly converted: "To be truthful, I thought it was a lot of nonsense. But when I arrived, it was

Paul Silas and Dave Cowens were anything but twin towers during their time together, but they regularly outhustled and outrebounded their taller opponents. A long day's journey into night followed Silas' departure from Boston.

amazing. It's almost like a collegiate atmosphere in a pro world, an atmosphere of total sacrifice for the good of the team, on and off the court. It's a way of life. You just fall into it."

With John Havlicek and Silas, Boston possessed two excellent forwards who earned All-Defensive honors that year to assist All-Star Dave Cowens. All-Star Jo Jo White continued to play great at guard with backcourt mate Don Chaney (another All-Defensive selection in 1972–73) with Don Nelson coming off the bench when needed as a sixth man. Always a very good defensive guard, Chaney posted personal bests in field goal and free throw percentage while scoring 1,000 points for the first time.

Red also drafted well, hauling in guard Paul Westphal, a USC grad like Bill Sharman. Unlike Sharman, the rookie did not excel at every sport he ever played nor did he ever don Dodgers blue, but this was one very good scoring guard. Terrific draft choice.

In many ways this team resembled the Celtics of a decade prior, allowing for some roster dilution due to league expansion—like any Celtics team of yore that lost only five games before Christmas, that is! And even though the team became a bit more vulnerable after the new year, it won eight more games than any other NBA team that season. This dominance extended into the Eastern Conference semis, as John Havlicek scored 54 points in the first contest and the Celtics rolled the Hawks in six to face the Knicks in the next round.

Yet it proved to be a false spring.

Think this team had smart players who understood team basketball? On Boston's roster this year were six future NBA head coaches: Don Nelson, Satch Sanders, Dave Cowens, Paul Westphal, Paul Silas, and Don Chaney. And who wouldn't have wanted John Havlicek as a coach if he was so inclined? Silas summed it up in speaking of Red Auerbach's influence over the organization: "Most of Red's players were intelligent players. It just kind of naturally followed that you stayed in something you loved. It was easy for most Celtics players to become coaches because of that tutelage and the way Red put things together."

In this era, the Celtics-Knicks rivalry rivaled the Red Sox–Yankees rivalry in intensity, with fans standing outside of Madison Square Garden for the sole purpose of abusing the Celtics players exiting the team bus, particularly Cowens. Ominously, although the Celtics dominated the regular season NBA schedule, they had tied their regular season series with the Knicks 4–4.

In the first two games, New York and Boston took turns blowing each other out, but the third game proved pivotal, not just because the Knicks won, but also because John Havlicek sustained a right shoulder injury fighting through a pick late in the game, this after leading all scorers. Postgame, Hondo needed the assistance of a trainer to cut the tape off his ankles.

Meanwhile, Dave DeBusschere continued to kill Boston, pouring in 17 points and taking Silas off his game. The Knicks' Phil Jackson, as is and was his custom, kept shooting his mouth off, but he and his teammates seemingly possessed the winning hand. Without Hondo, the Celtics lost Game 4 to fall behind in the series 3–1, as the refs called the Celtics for every foul imaginable. Groused Heinsohn, "When you play in New York, you've got to have a 20-point lead going into the fourth quarter. We had a 16-point lead, and that's why we lost." Jo Jo White concurred, "We were jobbed." Interestingly, these referees did not call any further games in this series.

Controversial refs aside, Havlicek returned for Game 5, scoring 18, virtually shooting everything left-handed, restoring Boston's pulse with a thrilling 98–97 win. Silas iced it with two free throws with seven seconds left. But Hondo was far from 100 percent, as he scored nine in a Game 6 win at Madison Square Garden, forcing a Game 7 in Boston. Luckily, Silas and Chaney excelled.

It all ended on April 29, with the Knicks holding Hondo to four points—hell, he could not even pick up the basketball at one juncture when it was lying on the court. Cowens and White played great, but the Knicks had too many healthy stars and a deep bench and won Game 7 to take the series. New York proceeded to defeat L.A. for the NBA title that year, a watershed event as thereafter they aged and declined rapidly into irrelevance. Since 1973, they have never won another championship.

Satch Sanders had played his last game as a Celtic, but he did not move far away, as Harvard University snapped him up as its new head basketball coach. Jo Jo White might have delivered the finest requiem for this heavyweight: "We have a lot of athletes in the pros. We don't have a lot of professionals. Professionalism has nothing to do with talent. It's those things that I was getting from Satch—how to listen, how to carry yourself, how to motivate your teammate, how you dress, how you talk to people. All these things are very, very important to people." Thomas "Satch" Sanders was elected to the National Basketball Hall of Fame in 2011 as a contributor, in part due to his founding of the NBA's Rookie Transition Program.

Led by their freshly crowned NBA Most Valuable Player Dave Cowens, the Celtics would eventually win another championship, and they did not have to wait too long to get it, either.

1973–74

They did not win 68 games in the new season, nor did they have to, comfortably winning the Atlantic Division by seven games over the Knicks; unlike the previous year, they lost only two games to their rivals. Despite the Knicks' decline and a fast Boston start, around the new year the Celtics (then 29–6) meandered into a malaise, or as president Jimmy Carter later defined it, a "crisis of…spirit." From this juncture until the conclusion of the regular season, this frustrating and frustrated bunch never won more than four in a row or lost more than two in a row. Unlike the 1972–73 season, when the Celtics rolled through their schedule, they now seemed rutted.

On a micro level, veterans began to openly question the managerial style of Tommy Heinsohn, much like Emmette Bryant and Larry Siegfried had once done, before those gentlemen entered the Land of the Lost. This time, though, dissension spread not from expendable players disgruntled with a first-year coach but from talented veterans exasperated that they were not playing at a championship level as the playoffs loomed.

In a weak draft that year, Boston picked Steve Downing from Indiana to spell Dave Cowens at center and then continued drafting players well after almost every other franchise dropped off, still calling out names in the 19th round. New blood provided little relief, so with the obvious exception of losing Satch Sanders, the Celtics entered the season by essentially having to play a pat hand, not that bad a predicament for a club that won 68 games.

At least one Celtic took a break. In late February, John Havlicek flew down to Florida to compete in the *Superstars* competition, a made-for-television event where various sports stars competed against each other for a purse of more than $100,000. Kyle Rote Jr. won that year, Hondo finishing well back and winning only $10,000. His downfall was bowling, where his balls went down the lane straight without bending at all. Hondo took it out on the Pistons after he returned, scoring 26 points and leading his team to a welcome win.

Dave Cowens ended the season second league-wide in rebounds per game, while Paul Silas bowled over intruders down low. Havlicek and Jo Jo White continued to excel, while Don Chaney and Don Nelson averaged 10.4 and 11.5 points per game, respectively. The team's three major scorers still played too many minutes per game, while Hank Finkel and Steve Downing almost wore grooves along the bench where they sat and sat and sat. Either management still did not know what it had with Paul Westphal, or it did not see the wisdom in increasing his minutes and resting some starters a bit.

Drawing the Buffalo Braves in the Eastern Conference semis, the Celtics had to go to six games to dispatch a 42–40 team in a surprisingly tough and bitter series. The Braves had some scorers in Bob McAdoo, Randy Smith, and Ernie DiGregorio and had defeated Boston in the final two matchups in their regular series. They had even waxed Kareem Abdul-Jabbar and the Bucks by 36 points once.

A largely forgotten series, Boston won in six only because its defense blunted a relentless offense. In the sixth game, the Celtics won by just two points as Jo Jo White iced it late with two free throws, but tellingly, neither he nor any of his teammates made a field goal in the last 8:12

of the game. The Braves had too many players who enjoyed scoring to justify that drought. But Boston endured to face New York in the Eastern Conference Finals.

What a difference a year makes. The Knicks collectively seemed to age 10 years in the span of one as the Celtics wiped them out in five games to advance to the NBA Finals against the Milwaukee Bucks. Estimable opponents Willis Reed, Jerry Lucas, and Dave DeBusschere had played their last games. One noteworthy series factoid: Dave Cowens set one record that survives to the present, the number of times a player was called "motherf*cker" by opposing fans in one playoff series.

Believing that they were seeing Dave DeBusschere for the final time, a respectful collection of Boston Celtics fans gave their nemesis a rousing ovation. To this day, Walt Frazier seemingly has not aged, Bill Bradley became a U.S. Senator, but the duller DeBusschere has become a forgotten man. In part, his dour personality got in his way, but this guy was a Celtic-killer, a shutdown defender, and a clutch shooter. His points-per-game average misleads, because so many of his shots came from three-point range before there were three-pointers. A few fans of a certain age recall that DeBusschere pitched for the Chicago White Sox—fewer still know the name of the pitcher the Pale Hose released to keep Dave on the mound for them: Denny McLain, the last man to win 30 major league games in one season.

Retired Bill Russell picked the Milwaukee Bucks to defeat the Celtics, and his prediction had a solid deductive basis; after all, they did have Hall of Famers Kareem Abdul-Jabbar and Oscar Robertson and a small forward named Bob Dandridge, who probably belongs in Springfield, too. A couple things Russ might have overlooked: Heinsohn knew how to coach, particularly in figuring out how to exploit an opponent's weaknesses, and the Bucks had many latent flaws, particularly in their backcourt with Lucius Allen hurting and Robertson past his prime.

Strategically, Heinsohn hounded Robertson by unleashing White and Chaney on him in smothering coverage, letting Silas handle Kareem and the rebounding, freeing Cowens to serve as the only center/shooting guard in the NBA and allowing his team to operate at a high level of emotion. Jabbar was a team player, not a one-man team, and Robertson no longer played at a superstar level. Knowing this, the crafty Heinsohn borrowed a page from an old Celtics playbook and kicked defenders out after Robertson, like K.C. Jones had once done. As soon as the Celtics neutralized Oscar, the defenders hounded Kareem.

The sixth game, a Celtics loss at the Garden, was the classic. Cowens, playing in foul trouble much of the game, fouled out, but with four seconds left in double OT, John Havlicek swished the apparent game winner. Unfortunately, Kareem converted a 15-foot hook shot at the other end of the court for the 102–101 victory. It was, said John Havlicek, "the best defense I've ever seen by two teams at the same time."

Then Boston won in the seventh game, a franchise tradition, having won three of their games in Milwaukee. Heinsohn had detected the Bucks' devotion to defending Hondo, so he directed Cowens to set picks and everyone else took advantage of the scoring opportunities. Jabbar had taken a Milwaukee team literally and figuratively on the brink of collapse (in the next two regular seasons they would win only 38 each of those years) to the seventh game of the Finals, but there his team fell prostrate to the Celtics at home 102–87.

Back in Boston, Cowens celebrated by sleeping the night away on the Common.

chapter 18

72 Bleeps and a '76 Banner

1974–75

Few people know this, but M.L. Carr suited up with the Celtics years before the complicated transaction that later brought him from Detroit to Boston. Originally drafted by the Kings, Kansas City–Omaha cut him, and the Celtics gave him a tryout, dropping him with Snake Jones (a man who wore a different hat every day, including a sombrero) as the final cuts before the 1974–75 campaign.

To his credit, Carr did not despair, instead catching on with the ABA, and five years later he scored 1,497 points with the Pistons while exuding positivity. Had the Celtics not cut him, they might have won the championship that year. Instead, other than adding a few rookies and an ABA castoff in center/forward Jim Ard, the Celtics kept their roster stable.

Funny story Paul Westphal told about his coach: "I'll always remember Tom Heinsohn's pep talks when I was with the Celtics. One time there were 72 bleeps in it—and it was Christmas Day."

Though not fully exploited, Paul Westphal improved greatly as a scorer, raising his points per game to 9.8 and finishing in the top 10 in the NBA in field goal percentage. Even better, Don Nelson led the NBA in shooting percentage. Westphal's emergence and Ard's addition proved fortuitous as Dave Cowens sustained a broken right foot and did not return to action until late November. With Ard and High Hank Finkel in the pivot, the team treaded water until Cowens returned, a couple of games over .500. As soon as he was back on the court, Cowens and his teammates rarely lost, eventually winning the Atlantic Division by 11 games.

George Thompson, the Celtic who never was, was drafted in 1969 but opted to play for the Pittsburgh Pipers in the ABA. He became a prolific scorer with the Pipers, Condors, Tams, and any other lame-named club in that league until it made peace with the NBA. Boston had the old rights but Thompson wanted to play in Wisconsin, where he had starred for Marquette, so Boston sold him to the Bucks, where he had a decent year and then never played basketball again.

In the Eastern Conference semifinals, Boston wiped the parquet floor with its opponent, a Houston Rockets team dependent on a few good scorers, a must for a defensively porous 41–41 squad. Boston's scorers, all of whom seemed hot, lit up their opponents like a Christmas tree.

Next they faced a Bullets team with an identical regular season record, one that had tied them in their series together, coached by K.C. Jones; because K.C. knew Celtics basketball and the plays never changed, at least one Boston player mused that it was like playing against a mirror. Theoretically then, the teams should have played seven games with the last one decided by one point.

Instead, Boston lost the first game at home and then did not break the Bullets in the second round at the Capital Center. Against an inferior opponent, the Celtics traditionally always came back, and though they did win two games, the team never regained a sense of momentum and bowed out in six.

For those old enough to remember, the outcome seemed vexing then and does not lend itself to a simple or pat analysis even today. The Bullets certainly had talented players—Wes Unseld and Elvin Hayes down low, Phil Chenier and Kevin Porter at guard, Mike Riordan and Nick Weatherspoon at small forward—and at times the Celts seemed to have them figured out. For example, in one game Paul Silas pulled down 25 boards against Washington's Twin Towers. The teams seemed about even, so it does not seem fair that the Bullets put Boston away with such relative ease.

Tommy Heinsohn sensed it early, declaring, "We beat ourselves again. We missed the shots, that's all.... We had the 15-footer, and we didn't make them." Don Chaney disappeared on offense too often and Paul Westphal had not fully impressed Red Auerbach and Heinsohn enough to get more minutes, so the club lost that potential spark. John Havlicek professed to the club being out of sync offensively, shots forced and plays not running well, but it still seemed unfathomable that the Bullets would have it so easy against the Celtics. It hurt too to see Golden State sweep Washington in the Finals; it was as if the Bullets had given up this great gift, a gift the Celtics gave them.

1975–76

The greatest game in NBA history and a championship!

Red always seemed to get the man who got away—this time it was Charlie Scott, who the team had drafted but had lost (or more accurately never had) to the ABA in 1970. In exchange, the Celtics parted with Westphal and two draft picks, placing a high value not just on Scott but on team toughness. Rumors abounded that Heinsohn and Westphal did not get along personally, yet this does not explain how Boston undervalued him, a player who then scored more than 20 points per game for the next five years for Phoenix. He also became one of the NBA's best playmakers on some not so great Suns teams.

Paul Westphal was standing in line at an airport with Charlie Scott directly behind him when players' union counsel Larry Fleischer informed Scott of his trade to Boston, pointing to Paul Westphal and explaining, "They just traded you for him."

Toughness is an oft-used cliché, but this trait statistically defined this team, with Scott leading the NBA in personal fouls and Cowens also in the "top" five in that category. Silas and Cowens finished 1-2 in offensive rebounds and top five overall in rebounding. Not that finesse disappeared entirely—after all, Jo Jo White still swished baskets—but this club placed three players on the league's All-Defensive team in Cowens, Silas, and Havlicek.

Here is a tangible example of the team's toughness and approach: in late February the Rockets' Mike Newlin flopped twice, causing the refs to call fouls on an exasperated Dave Cowens. Deciding to exact some frontier justice, Cowens lasered in on Newlin, driving down the right side of the court, then ran over to the Rocket, and with both hands, lifted the flopper off into the Celtics bench. Cowens then addressed one of the refs, "Now *that's* a [bleeping] foul!"

Expecting to face the Warriors (59–23) in the NBA Finals, Boston blasted through the first two rounds only to face the Phoenix Suns, a 42–40 regular season squad that had very improbably upset Rick Barry and teammates. Other than Paul Westphal and Rookie of the Year Alvan Adams, the Suns did not radiate much talent, and Boston had defeated them all four times they had played that year.

Yet after four games, the Suns had squared the series 2–2 with the rather indignant Celtics forced to tame these upstarts at the Garden exactly a month before the country's bicentennial. When there though, Phoenix failed to create fireworks, falling behind 36–18 after Celtics backup center Jim Ard converted a jumper. By half, Boston led 61–45.

During the intermission, the fans basked in the apparent blowout, content to make fun of color commentator Rick Barry's alleged hair. Unbeknownst to Celtics Nation, their shooters had grown cold, and in the third period their shooting reflected it. The Suns improbably tied the game, though the Celts did regain the lead at 77–72, with Silas and Scott bleeding fouls.

That margin of five points stood with less than a minute remaining in regulation, until expatriate Paul Westphal, smothered by double coverage, sank a turnaround jump shot. Then he torched Boston on defense, batting away the ball from a dribbling Charlie Scott to Alvan Adams, who ricocheted it back to a fast-breaking Westphal. Scott fouled out, making contact with Westphal, who nevertheless scored. He tied it with his free throw, and Boston got collectively tighter than the reins on Paul Revere's horse.

It kept getting worse as Jo Jo missed a jumper and Cowens fouled Curtis Perry. Perry made his first free throw but thankfully missed his second attempt as a highly anxious Boston regained the ball with 22 seconds left, behind by one.

Hondo took the inbound pass at half-court and Adams slapped him, fouling out. Like Perry a moment earlier, Havlicek sank the first free throw and missed the second, but this time Boston got the rebound with the score tied. Unfortunately, Havlicek took an errant shot, and Phoenix got the ball back with three seconds left.

The Suns' Gar Heard heaved it in, but Cowens intercepted, and time ran out with the game going into overtime tied at 95–95.

In OT, with 29 seconds left in a 101–101 tie, Phoenix inbounded the ball, and Adams' replacement, Dennis Awtrey, was fouled. Phoenix could play for the last shot but confoundingly it did not, and their "last shot" missed as Silas rebounded it with three seconds left and promptly called a timeout. Don Nelson then inbounded to Havlicek, who faked out Gar Heard but then missed the clear shot as Nelson sprinted unsuccessfully through the baseline to tap it in. Double overtime had come to the Hub, and some of its fans were drunk or mean. Or both.

Jo Jo White had kept Boston competitive all night, and he played only with more intensity after Cowens fouled out, leading his team once again to a 109–106 Celtics lead. The lead crumbled with Phoenix scoring four straight, yet the Celtics had the ball back with five seconds left to end the ordeal. Havlicek heaved the ball, looking as if he would fall over forward in the process, and his shot swished in. Fans ran onto the parquet and after Celtics players, who in turn plunged toward their locker room to escape their fans.

In the midst of this spontaneous exhibition of communal relief, referee Richie Powers raised two of his fingers, signifying that two seconds remained in overtime. Some knucklehead fan then assaulted and battered

Powers, but he had made the correct call and those fans who had not committed a crime returned to their seats and the players went back to work.

Richie Powers was not the first NBA official assaulted by Boston droogs after a playoff game. On April 24, 1966, after a four-point loss to the Lakers at the Garden, a gaggle of idiots confronted refs Earl Strom and Norm Drucker as they walked to their dressing rooms. Only the timely intervention by several Boston police officers prevented further violence and likely serious injuries from occurring.

Out of timeouts, Paul Westphal called one for Phoenix anyway in order to incur a technical foul and get the inbound pass at half-court, which was the rule at the time. Jo Jo White extended his team's lead by two by sinking the foul shot, but now Phoenix had the inbound under

In one of the greatest basketball games ever played, John Havlicek led the Celtics to a triple-overtime victory over the Phoenix Suns in Game 5 of the 1976 NBA Finals.

more advantageous circumstances. Taking advantage, Phoenix's Gar Heard took the inbound pass, turned, and drained the shot just before time expired. Triple overtime: 112–112.

In foul trouble most of the evening, Paul Silas fouled out at 3:23, replaced by Glenn McDonald and perhaps the same spirit that had guided Gene Guarilia so many years ago against the Lakers. McDonald tallied six points in the third overtime but also made a key rebound. Dave Cowens' replacement, Jim Ard, converted two free throws for a six-point Celtic lead, though Westphal threatened to force a fourth overtime by making two baskets to pull the Suns to within two points. As he had consistently done, Jo Jo White took the inbound pass and he dribbled the life out of the Suns as finally the game ceased. The exhausted White scored 33 points and played every minute.

After the game Suns GM Jerry Colangelo demanded better security at the Boston Garden if the series went to seven games, but it never did. Anticlimactically, the Celtics won the sixth and deciding game in Phoenix, entitling them to another championship banner.

Don Nelson, the most reliable of Celtics, announced his retirement in January and ended his career in Boston on a high, having scored 20 points to seal victory for his team on his farewell night. No one shouted out, "We love you Nellie," but his basketball acumen led him to a Hall of Fame NBA coaching career thereafter.

Jo Jo White won the Jack Barry Sportsmanship Award, a newly minted distinction honoring the late *Boston Globe* sportswriter who had reported on the Celtics from the franchise's inception. Poor Jack somehow covered the team without ever learning to drive, but because everyone liked him, he always managed to get to the arena or high school gym.

The celebrations in the locker room had hardly gotten started when Paul Silas observed, "I just remembered something. My contract's up this year, isn't it? Hmmmmm."

chapter 19

No Ws and Ls
on Our Paychecks

1976–77

On October 20, 1976, the Boston Celtics might have committed their worst trade in franchise history, as they swung a three-team deal in which they gave up Paul Silas for Curtis Rowe.

Curtis Rowe?

Even the most dedicated Red Auerbach apologist cannot defend this move, essentially one borne out of stinginess, the senseless sacrifice of one of the ultimate team players for one of the least team-oriented players. And earlier, they had bought Sidney Wicks from the Trail Blazers, a red flag right there; who sells a player instead of trading for equal value or a number of high draft picks? And why be cheap with a quality guy like Silas and then spend money on Wicks?

All summer Silas and his agent had clashed with Auerbach, even unsuccessfully resorting to arbitration. The dedication and hard-nosed play that characterized the reigning champions evaporated, as the team embraced fantasy league players whose sense of entitlement and self-worth never approached reality. Arguably, Auerbach is the finest coach and general manager in basketball history, but he created this mess, a bitter lesson that he learned and profited from when it came time to negotiate with Larry Bird.

Supposedly, Rowe and Wicks, two former UCLA Bruins, knew how to play together, and their presence would transform a weakness at the forward position to a formidable bulwark. It did not work well, as the team lost four straight after winning their first four. Then it turned ugly.

Often a few strides ahead of the rest of the NBA, Red Auerbach tried out Drazen Dalipagic, a star Yugoslavian player in advance of the 1976–77 season. As Dalipagic later related, "Auerbach was so convinced that I would stay that he called John Havlicek, a living legend in Boston, and introduced me to him saying: 'This is your heir!' John was really kind to me, gave me a lot of support, but the circumstances didn't allow me to stay." Circumstances? "It may look impossible or ridiculous nowadays, but back them there was no relationship between FIBA and the NBA. We had amateur status in Europe, and all relationships with the professional world were banned. I thought about it for some days and I decided not to accept the offer because I couldn't imagine not playing again for my country, and I don't regret that decision." Dalipagic was inducted into the Basketball Hall of Fame in Springfield in 2004, and had he stuck with Boston, would have been the first European player in the NBA and conceivably might have won some titles here as well.

On November 11, what World War I vets always referred to as Armistice Day, a battle erupted as the Celtics announced that Dave Cowens had taken a leave of absence. Cowens explained his decision repeatedly over the next few weeks but basically he had "burned out," or at least that became the party line.

Because Cowens has always enjoyed adulation and in many quarters unconditional love in Boston, most people forgave him for his absence, excusing the act without understanding it. Dave being Dave. Most of the same group of fans who excoriated Wicks and Rowe did not see fit to even require Cowens to utter two Our Fathers and three Hail Marys, hypocrisy reduced to its most fundamental elements. All three players hurt the Celtics, Wicks and Rowe for what they did on the court, Cowens for not even being on the court at all. At least Wicks and Rowe suited up.

He did return, but by then the defending champs sported a 19–19 record and the rot had really set in. Plus, the game before Cowens' return,

Charlie Scott hit the floor and bent his left wrist backward, breaking it so badly that he missed 34 games. Wicks and Rowe did not perform harmoniously with their teammates, or particularly effectively with each other, although on given nights they could overpower their opponents. They were locker room cankers. At one point, Charlie Scott supposedly blew up at Wicks, pointing out, "The trouble is *him*! He's not a Celtic." Actually, the trouble was that Wicks *was* a Celtic, just not one cut out of the proud tradition of winners. So quickly had the Celtics mystique evaporated, that they whiffed on signing washed-up guard Dean "the Dream" Meminger.

Sidney Wicks possesses one of the statistically oddest careers in NBA history. In his rookie year he scored more than 2,000 points, but with the exception of one year, he scored between 100 and 300 fewer points each season thereafter in his 10 years of service. His free throw percentages during that time show more variation, as he started with a .710 and got as high as .762 in his third year but ended with an awful .507.

Amid the tumult and mediocre record, this team made the playoffs, defeating the Spurs in the first round. Jo Jo White led in scoring in each game, and even Wicks and Rowe contributed. In the Eastern Conference semis the Celtics drew the Philadelphia 76ers and lost in seven games, a result that either was very good, all things considered, or very disappointing given that they bowed early in their title defense.

They had a team of All-Stars (John Havlicek, Cowens, White, Rowe, and Wicks had all been selected at least once), just like the 2011 Boston Red Sox, with the same absence of cohesion or sense of purpose. Sheer talent squired them into the playoffs, but this team stood poised on the edge of an abyss, an ugly team on the verge of becoming a hopelessly divided one.

Outside of the Garden, the advent of busing in the Boston Public Schools, first instituted in the fall of 1974, had created an image for Boston as the most racist city in the country. Soon, the Garden walls could not contain the hatred.

1977–78

Johnny Most or the fan who yelled out "We love you, Cooz" might have the most recognizable quotes in Celtics history, but the player who uttered perhaps the most infamous quote is Curtis Rowe, who allegedly said after a loss, "Come on, fellas, there ain't no Ws and Ls on our paychecks!" Or some variation of the theme. That quote summed up the utter lack of team cohesion and unity to achieve common goals.

Looking back on his rookie experience, Cedric Maxwell said in *Sports Illustrated,* "My first season here we had seven guys who were All-Stars. We had more talent than we do now—superstars at every position—but a lot of them were misfits. Just because you put five guys together on the floor doesn't mean they're going to play well together."

Foreshadowing the tumultuous year awaiting them, the Celtics lost out on obtaining small forward John Johnson, a deal that they seemingly had consummated in June. Even as a reserve, Johnson was a valuable teammate to have around, a player who generally scored around 1,000 points per season and seemed to enjoy playing basketball. This team needed this.

Stranded on the Island of Misfit Toys, this Celtics edition bolted out to a 1–8 start, failing to score at least 100 points on three occasions. Auerbach dumped poor Norm Cook, Steve Kuberski, and Jim Ard, but these sacrificial lambs made little impression on the players who really were killing this team.

Remember the team that played on Christmas but whose families got together that morning at Satch Sanders' house? Not a trace of it remained, and at the team's Christmas party, only the families of John Havlicek and Jo Jo White attended; poignantly at the end, Red Auerbach gathered the unopened presents and took them away. This assemblage of individuals had to be blown up.

In this vein, just missing the Christmas rush, on December 27 Auerbach traded Charlie Scott to the Lakers for Kermit Washington, old friend Don Chaney, and a first-round draft choice (which Boston later used to pick Freeman Williams). Kermit Washington, serving a 60-day suspension for throwing a punch into the kisser of Rudy Tomjanovich, might have helped this team. By all accounts, that action was out of character for him, and by this time, the forward and sometimes center had worked himself into becoming one of the better defenders in the league, one of the best offensive rebounders, and a top-10 field goal percentage shooter. Chaney, a popular returnee to the Hub, had largely lost what scoring touch he once possessed but still defended, though with reduced minutes.

No trade could fix the Celtics, though, with Jo Jo White suffering through a sore left heel that ultimately required surgery, ending his season with almost 1,000 fewer points than the year before, a huge loss to the team in leadership and production. At this point the club had reeled off another skein of losses and largely ignored Tommy Heinsohn.

If ever asked to name all the Celtics in the Basketball Hall of Fame, never forget the estimable Dave Bing, who played his final season in Boston. Bing had starred previously mostly with the Pistons, scoring 2,000 points or more on two occasions while invariably seizing a spot as one of the league leaders in assists, a point guard before there was such a thing. He not only provided leadership and a sense of stability on a club often lacking in players possessing those attributes but also played a lot of minutes in the absence of Jo Jo White. Bing's experience with this rambunctious team provided him with valuable experience for his current role as mayor of Detroit, Michigan.

Finally, after the new year (Auerbach did not want to ruin the holidays) the team fired Tommy Heinsohn, replacing him as coach with Satch Sanders and persuading K.C. Jones to serve as an assistant coach on the team.

In explaining the changes, Auerbach stated, "I went to practices and practically pleaded with the players. But after I left the situation would be the same." Larry Whiteside of the *Boston Globe* eulogized Heinsohn as "a man caught up in the tidal wave of change in the NBA.... He just withered and fell to the ground..."

Red delivered an ultimatum to some of the underperforming players, informing them, "We're going to start winning, or some of you will be gone. Even if I have to give you away." But then, days later, he admitted that he might retire himself, the firing of Heinsohn constituting the most "traumatic" event of his life.

Initially, many people welcomed the ascension of Satch Sanders; he knew his basketball intricately, he was hip and cool, and he might "communicate" with his charges better than had Heinsohn, a man now seemingly less relevant to Boston than the crew cut hairstyle he popularized as a player.

For Satch, the honeymoon barely lasted a week, with Wicks whining, "I feel a trade is imminent.... I think it might be the best solution for all parties." Suddenly, Satch had become less relevant to Boston than Tommy Heinsohn. It was a great honeymoon, honey. Now can we get divorced? Opined John Powers, to the Celtics came "the cold realization that a coaching change does not immediately bring miracles."

Auerbach executed some minor moves, trading Fred Saunders to the Jazz for a second-rounder and signing Ernie DiGregorio, Zaid Abdul-Aziz, and Bob Bigelow to free agent contracts, but though the club played a bit better for Sanders than it had for Heinsohn, it did not play particularly well and continued to comfortably lose more than it won.

Seemingly the Celtics had cornered the market on the underperforming and divisive, but then Red would surprise everyone by trading some of the malcontents to other franchises for their sourpusses. Regardless, the team ended up with a 32–50 record.

Auerbach at one point suggested selecting Sidney Wicks as the team's Unsung Hero, undoubtedly concluding that his ass had not been kissed enough.

John Havlicek retired. Who could blame him?

Undaunted, Red Auerbach selected Indiana State's junior forward, a kid named Larry Bird, in that spring's NBA draft.

chapter 20

Kentucky Fried Disaster

1978–79

He had never seen Boston Garden or even possessed any inkling what it looked like, but in mid-summer Buffalo Braves owner (and the co-owner who made Kentucky Fried Chicken a national staple) John Y. Brown traded ownership of his franchise for Irv Levin's Boston Celtics. It was Brown's third franchise in three years, as he previously had folded his Kentucky Colonels rather than pay the NBA entrance fee for merging ABA clubs. Irv Levin was not a good owner; John Y. was an extremely poor one.

Could the Clippers hang 13 Celtics championship banners from high above courtside at the Staples Center in Los Angeles? Arguably yes, because Celtics owner Irv Levin moved his team to the West Coast, compelled to honor deferred contracts with past Celtics players thereafter, payable by Clippers checks. In essence, Levin moved the Celtics out west and changed their name but did not alter the team's lineal ties to Honey Russell's original club. As a product of the uncertainty, Tom Heinsohn filed suit in federal court so that he did not have to coach for the Clippers, because there was interest in "rehiring" him under his Celtics contract. Or in the alternative, for those remaining Buffalo Braves fans, take comfort—it is possible that your favorite basketball team never died. It just metamorphosed into the Boston Celtics. Confused? Some Celtics players wanted to renegotiate under the theory that a newly minted Boston Celtics team now had to negotiate with them as free agents.

Levin promptly moved the Braves to San Diego (renamed the Clippers, they later moved to L.A.) and announced the trade of Nate Archibald,

Marvin Barnes, Billy Knight, and draft picks to the Celtics for Kevin Kunnert, Kermit Washington, Sidney Wicks, and Freeman Williams. Classlessly, Levin bragged that he had swindled Brown. Certainly Williams posted a couple of good years in San Diego, but Archibald surprisingly revived his career in Boston and the Celtics later parlayed one of the draft picks into the rights to Danny Ainge. Most important, the club had puked out Wicks once and for all. Advantage, John Y.

Except at this point, Red Auerbach had not decided to stay in Boston any longer, as the Knicks offered him money and ownership and were not interested in upstaging or ignoring him, something John Y. Brown cared little about. So Red flew to New York to meet with Knicks owner Sonny Werblin and had all but signed a contract with his longtime opponents when he decided to remain a Celtic. It had been close as Red emphasized: "That stuff about me leaving was not a figment of anyone's imagination. The contract was drawn up, and the money was far in excess of what I was making."

Legend has that a local cabdriver talked Red out of leaving town, which of course does not explain why Red did not order the cabbie to turn around and save him a flight to Gotham and back. Most likely this kindly and avuncular cabbie existed about as much as Manti Te'o's fake girlfriend; Red's wife, Dot, surmised his mixed feelings and said, "Arnold, you are a Boston Celtic. You are not a New York Knick. You either go back to Boston or come home. You are a Celtic or you are retired." Had he fully appreciated what awaited him, Red would have either signed up with the Knicks or retired, because John Y. Brown proved to be the anti–Walter Brown.

Unsurprisingly, after the season commenced, the Celtics won only two of their first 14 games, and by mid-November, the ax fell on Satch Sanders. Dave Cowens became player/coach.

Having dumped some train wrecks, the Celtics had to cope with some new ones, the most vexing being former Providence star Marvin Barnes. An immensely talented man, he starred his first two years in the old ABA, a rookie of the year with the Spirits, but he had exhibited cockeyed behavior before coming to Boston. This descent only escalated when he got to the Garden, and after missing several practices, Cowens exclaimed, "I don't want him around. I don't want him in uniform in the building." Promptly afterward, Marvin Barnes left the building never to return—as a player at least.

Earlier, Boston had traded Jo Jo White to the Warriors for a first-round draft choice, heralding the termination of a great Celtics career. The team's iron man had consistently placed the fortunes of the team ahead of his own physical ailments, shortening his career and marring his chances of induction to the Basketball Hall of Fame.

The club also swapped Billy Knight even up for center Rick Robey.

The Celtics were springing leaks, literally as well as figuratively. In a further sign of franchise decline, in a game in January the roof of the Garden became a sieve, dripping water into a bucket near one of the baskets.

Unwisely, owner John Y. Brown then traded away this future draft choice and two others, along with Tom Barker, for center/forward Bob McAdoo, reportedly to please his wife, former Miss America Phyllis George. Deadpanned Auerbach later, "What are you gonna do? Criticize the owner? Besides, people wouldn't have believed me if I told them how dumb this guy was."

The opposite of Mr. Congeniality, McAdoo had lost some of his scoring touch and proved a disruption to the clubhouse, having squandered his honeymoon period after a month of service. He did not appear to enjoy playing for Coach Cowens, playing eight fewer minutes per game than he had with the Knicks. From the outside, Indiana State's Larry Bird supposedly asked questions about the McAdoo deal. The losses continued.

Auerbach had once quit when an owner went over his head, like Ben Kerner did to him back with the old Tri-Cities Hawks in the 1940s. Red had not mellowed; he simply figured out how to position his adversaries to hang themselves. In the meantime, Red had to bite his lip often around John Y. For instance, after another Boston loss, John Y. verbally accosted Auerbach, saying, "Here comes our great leader now. Say something intelligent, great leader." Only one type of person says something like this, but Red ducked a rare fight here, knowing ultimately that when he chose to fight John Y. it would be a knife fight.

Meanwhile, the Celtics hit their nadir on March 9, when they lost 160–117 to a Pistons team almost as poor as they were. From there, the club closed out the season winning only four of its last 17 games.

Amid all of the controversy generated by John Y., one critical factor escaped most fans' notice: the man had a partner in Harry Mangurian, and to the rapturous cries for salvation of Celtics fans, he responded by buying out John Y., who wanted to become governor of Kentucky anyway. It was either John Y. or Auerbach, as Red issued an ultimatum, having endured all of the senseless interference and insults that meandered out of John Y. Brown's big misinformed mouth.

By late March, John Y. saw the future of Celtics basketball, and it was not him, admitting, "I may well sell out of the basketball team in Boston because I don't have that much interest in it." In response, Auerbach grunted, "That's up to him." Cowens was ecstatic: "That's the best news I've heard all year. Go ahead. What do I care if he's leaving?"

The erstwhile Kentucky Fried Chicken king sold his interest to Harry Mangurian and left Boston, and damned if John Y. did not become governor. By this time few cared, as Mangurian kept Auerbach in Boston and began to rebuild.

Having blown the Paul Silas negotiations, Auerbach negotiated in hard-nosed fashion with Larry Bird's agent, Bob Woolf, but Woolf knew Red had to bend in the end. Too much of a mess remained from the loss of Silas, and Boston fans might have stormed the Garden had Bird called Red's bluff and not signed. Bird got a lucrative contract, and the clouds began parting. Happy days were here again.

chapter 21

The Hick from French Lick

1979–80

The Celtics had unwisely let M.L. Carr slip past them years ago, but Red Auerbach regretted the decision and now coveted the gifted swingman who had just scored 1,497 points, finishing second-team All-Defensive and second league-wide in minutes played per game. Unlike many of the grouches who had graced the Celtics roster for the previous two years, Carr was and is an extremely positive man, a key feature in transforming a team of whiners into winners.

Trouble was, Detroit did not want to see him go, so its execs got into a scrap with Auerbach, which was never a good idea. At the conclusion of negotiations, the Celtics had not only obtained Carr but had shipped out Bob McAdoo to the Pistons for two first-round draft picks, a neat reversal of the horrendous trade that brought McAdoo to Boston in the first place.

That solved some problems—the hiring of Bill Fitch as coach solved many more. Fitch had devoted the 1970s to coaching the Cleveland Cavaliers, weaning them from their expansion year through nine seasons, their finest ending in the spring of 1976 when they lost to the Celtics in the Eastern Conference Finals in six games. The Celtics team Fitch took over resembled an expansion team as well, with a super rookie surrounded by players who had built up a history.

In that vein, he zeroed in on Curtis Rowe, not caring for his lack of fitness, and canned him on the first day of veteran camp. Despite

Auerbach having pledged to ban Rowe, the prodigal forward had returned, if only to serve as a foil for the new no-nonsense coach. Fitch was hard-nosed, and although it would take five different teams to prove that his coaching tenure always parabolically rose before precipitously falling, all Boston cared about was seeing the ascent.

Fresh off becoming one of the more wealthy young men in America, Larry Bird then took a step toward humility by entering the gates to the Celtics rookie camp at Camp Milbrook in Marshfield, Massachusetts, owned by team exec Jan Volk's father, Jerry. Red Auerbach toodled around in a golf cart while coaches watched draft choices scrimmage against not only each other but collegians and some veteran Celtics trying to get into shape. The prospects played on hardtop outdoor courts, slept in bunks, and ate camp food. They did everything but roast marshmallows as they permanently left their boyhoods behind, and for most, their boyhood dreams of becoming a professional ballplayer.

Besides Bird, another rookie, Gerald Henderson, had survived rookie camp (and the subsequent special camp for the 10 best rookies/free agents, a new innovation), impressing Fitch and Auerbach enough to earn a spot on the roster. Drafted by San Antonio a year earlier and waived, the young guard did not play at all in the NBA, then fortuitously fell into the lap of a team in bad need of guards, with little depth behind Nate Archibald and Chris Ford other than a seemingly very old Don Chaney. The club drafted a host of guards, but it had no picks until the third round and kept only Wayne Kreklow.

Up front it looked much brighter, with Dave Cowens and Rick Robey (swapped last season straight up for Billy Knight) at center, surrounded by forwards Bird, Carr, and Cedric Maxwell. A roster that had appeared so disjointed and hapless had taken shape into something positive very quickly under Fitch, particularly with Auerbach restoring his proven formula of accumulating Celtics types of players, instead of feeding the monster with erstwhile All-Stars.

Armed with this new approach, instead of opening the season at 2–8, this Celtics edition surged to an 8–2 start. The previous year, when Fitch coached in Cleveland, the Cavaliers had defeated the Celtics by 14 points in the first game of the season at the Garden. This year, Boston played the Cavs in the second and third games and won by 22 and 19 points, respectively. Far from an aggregation of misfits, the Celtics blew out teams such as the Bullets and the Nets with embarrassing ease while competing successfully against clubs such as the Lakers and the Sixers, winning the Atlantic Division with a 61–21 record.

For the second straight year, Cedric Maxwell led the NBA in field goal percentage (.609) while scoring almost 17 points per night. Nate Archibald, once an unbelievable scorer and the only man in NBA history to lead one season in points scored and assists, moderated his petulance and became a very effective point guard under Fitch, second overall in the league in assists while adding 14.1 points per game. Chris Ford also distinguished himself, finishing second in the NBA in three-point percentage while accepting a lesser scoring role overall.

In assessing Larry Bird, you almost have to look at a different aspect of his performance each year, like Bill Russell, to get an adequate overall assessment of his greatness. He scored 21.3 points per game in his Rookie of the Year season but also ended up top 10 in defensive rebounds and total rebounds. Even Larry Bird experienced growing pains—some games he did not shoot well, and in others he got torched on defense—but generally he posted one of the greatest rookie seasons ever. He could have shirked his rebounding duties, but to his credit he did not and instead decided how to excel in this aspect of his game.

The team added another guard in January, future Hall of Famer Pete Maravich, a terrific acquisition who scored 11.5 per game down the stretch. Having survived an overbearing father, a wicked drug habit, and unreal expectations, Pistol Pete faced his stiffest test when he heard Johnny Most's voice on a regular basis, something he did not fully appreciate until he joined the club.

Even without his glasses, retired Celtics superstar John Havlicek would have had no trouble discerning the greatness of No. 33, Larry Bird. Neither Havlicek nor Bird ever left any unexpended effort on the court during their careers.

In the semifinals, the Celtics swept the Houston Rockets, who at the time were still playing in the Eastern Conference, with the closest margin a 17-point rout in the fourth and deciding game. Boston then faced Julius Erving and the 76ers in the Eastern Conference Finals, a team that had split their six regular season matchups. Frankly, the Celtics did not match up very well with them and bowed out in five games.

Offensively, the team scored fewer than 98 points in every single game against the Sixers, losing two games at the Garden. With the exception of the last game, Bird dominated the scoring for the Celtics, and though each game was close, perhaps if Fitch had played Maravich more, they might have squeaked by to play the Lakers. Maybe.

But Pistol Pete never specialized in blocking shots or clearing bodies down low, and Boston did not have enough help there to contain Julius Erving enough to win. The Celtics frontcourt held the key to their future fortune; they simply did not have enough yet.

For the superstitious in Celtics Nation, Boston never had a chance in Larry Bird's rookie season, particularly after a mirror in the dressing room during the Eastern Conference Finals fell, injuring M.L. Carr and Gerald Henderson.

The fairy-book season for Larry Bird did not materialize. Dazzled by the success of the new-look Celtics team, fans expected perhaps a bit too much from a group that had started camp with Curtis Rowe. It was disappointing, but next year Bird would have a year of experience to draw on, and much more important, the Boston Garden beckoned his two new partners in the frontcourt.

chapter 22

Kevin and Robert Walk through the Door

1980–81

Joe Barry Carroll was one of the men most responsible for the Celtics' three titles in the next six years, an unsung hero. Carroll was the first player chosen in the 1980 NBA draft, a future All-Star (once) and one of the league's leading scorers for the first six years of his career. The Golden State Warriors, to get his rights (and a later first-round pick), traded their veteran center, Robert Parish, and the third choice overall to Boston. With that third overall pick, the Celtics drafted Kevin McHale of the University of Minnesota. In Boston, even if you did not own a BayBanks card, life just kept getting better.

Red Auerbach still had some personnel headaches even after completing this coup. McHale threatened to sign with an Italian team, flying over to Milan to either play there or jack up his value in Boston. In other developments, Tiny Archibald threatened not to re-sign, and although he and McHale both obviously did report, Pistol Pete Maravich announced his retirement.

Maravich's retirement struck some fans nestled in a more nostalgic era, the now–grown-ups who had devoured articles about him with provocative titles like "Pistol Pete and the Press," or wore oversized droopy white socks and tried to replicate his moves. But he was not really a Celtic. Dave Cowens was, and when he retired shortly thereafter, a theatrical curtain closed. Although grown men and women might not have cried, they felt really bad about this. He was one of us, a funny regular guy, and Boston fans would not come to feel this way about another player until they got to know Kevin McHale.

For residents of the West Roxbury district of Boston, the Celtics' finest pick might have been guard Ronnie Perry. An All-American in baseball, he was drafted both by the Red Sox and later the White Sox. He never played in the majors—though he was involved in a trade for Jerry Koosman—and might have played in Boston had Nate Archibald extended his holdout. Years after Perry moved out of Westie, residents still reverently point to his boyhood home or his retired jersey in the gym, remembering nights when he shot the lights out, and after the postgame parties had ended, they fell to sleep thinking that one day they might see Perry on the parquet at the Boston Garden, much as they had entertained the same dreams about themselves not so very long before.

The Kevin McHale who almost played in Italy infuriated Auerbach and Bill Fitch—why was this guy not running to sign a contract for much less than recent No. 3 draft picks or for a bit more than half of what Larry Bird signed for the year before? Hard man to figure out, this ingrate from Minnesota. When he arrived in camp, McHale swatted back shots and confirmed what many NBA scouts had figured out, that Auerbach had dropped two spaces in the draft to pick the best player out there, the only future Hall of Famer available that year.

Oddly, even though Robert Parish had already played four years for Golden State, where he pulled down more than 700 rebounds (scoring 17 points per game the previous season), he presented much more of a puzzle than McHale. The Chief had acquired a reputation, deserved or undeserved, as an underachiever and a partier, and folks like that had run through Celtics coaches in the late 1970s like a scythe. In Boston, Parish had to compete against Rick Robey for the starting center's job—nothing came guaranteed.

Acquired by Red Auerbach in an astute trade with Golden State, Robert Parish was a nine-time All-Star and three-time champion in Boston.

Before the regular season began, Dave Cowens announced his retirement in a letter to the fans, where he stated in part, "the majority of the folks who are serious viewers would recognize the tremendous talent of the players who are continuing to demonstrate their skills and would see I am not able to perform against these players in the manner I would want to and in the manner the fan expects me to. I hope I am correct in my assumption because I would not want anyone to get even remotely upset." Previously, he had announced his decision to his teammates on a bus taking them to an exhibition game in Indiana against the Bulls. At the end, M.L. Carr loudly deadpanned, "Well, get off our bus!" His teammates laughed, but they felt as bittersweet to see Cowens depart as any fan, appreciative that they had seen one of the finest of sportsmen.

The team drove Fitch nuts at the beginning, an unmolded congregation: Bird's shots and passing too often went awry; Gerald Henderson scored at the expense of playmaking; and Parish had not quite dug into the low post with the same intensity as had Cowens. One bright spot was Kevin McHale, who drew raves for his defense, seemingly coming out of nowhere to block shots or challenge opponents, a trait not much commented upon since Bill Russell had retired.

Good early Larry Bird story: in a game against the Pacers he ran over the opposing guard, a diminutive Jerry Sichting. At least one journalist questioned if the takedown harked back to some type of college bad blood, to which Bird replied, "Nothing like that. I just let him know I didn't want any little guard coming down and setting a pick on me." As a measure of Larry Bird's intensity on the floor, this game did not even count—it occurred in the preseason.

But then a "home" win at the Hartford Civic Center against the Bulls on November 9 sparked a six-game winning streak, and then a month later a 12-game winning streak (then a 13-game streak to start the new year) demonstrated to fans and foes alike what the 1980s were going to be like for Celtics Nation, as the team won 62 games.

Back then the Celtics had to play some home games at the Hartford Civic Center, and at times they seemed to be hexed there. In 1980–81, for example, this club, which won more than 75 percent of its games, lost three out of five in Hartford. Finally, the roof fell in at the Civic Center, but contrary to vicious rumors, no Celtic was involved.

In the playoffs, Boston swept the Bulls in the Eastern Conference semifinals for the privilege of participating in the series every basketball fan relished, the rematch with Philadelphia. Even though Boston had technically won the Atlantic Division, it had again tied its series with the 76ers, and each team finished at 62–20. This was not last year's Sixers; in the draft they had picked up dangerous shooting guard Andrew Toney.

This series resembled the matchup from the previous year, as Boston fell behind 3–1, losing one game by missing way too many free throws. Apparently Julius Erving was not only Dr. J, he was the Celtics' daddy.

Cockeyed optimists might point to the fact that Philly had won the first game by only one point and the fourth by two. These two teams were extraordinarily evenly matched, so it stood to reason that matters would even out. Maybe, but things looked really bad.

Evenly matched but different, Cedric Maxwell began tailing Dr. J with success, but even more important the team figured a way to defuse Andrew Toney. Parish controlled down low and Larry Bird and Nate Archibald sparked even more plays, and with these improvements, the Celtics evened the series by winning the fifth and sixth games, each by two points. Fitch adroitly exploited his bench, with McHale shining in the sixth game with 14 points and five rebounds in the fourth quarter alone.

Game 7. Fitch's game plan was simple: neutralize Erving, a player who had blown out 31 candles on his birthday cake and had played in every regular season game (plus a two-game mini-series against the Pacers and seven games in the Eastern semis against the Bucks) and now had gone the distance with Boston. Max harassed him, and every time Erving got the ball, other Celtics swarmed him, too.

It almost did not work. Archibald rang up some early fouls, so Gerald Henderson had to round out the second period for him, performing his task well. Philly led late in the second 53–48, so Fitch pulled Bird and replaced him with Eric Fernsten; the Celtics had a foul to give, so Fernsten, following Fitch's orders, fouled Dr. J with two seconds on the clock, keeping the game within five for Boston at the half.

The previous season, a mirror had ominously fallen on M.L. Carr and Gerald Henderson, foreshadowing the Celtics' demise. This year, in the sixth game at Philly, a fan stabbed Cedric Maxwell with a pencil, causing Max to seek out his assailant and erase him.

Watch this game if you can find a recording of it. The 1980s were not simply the Celtics versus Lakers, Bird against Magic, because the Sixers played excellent basketball until 1987, two years after Andrew Toney's promising career fell off. But that had not happened yet.

In the third quarter, the Celtics looked finished, with Robert Parish consigned to the bench with four fouls. The team had fallen behind by 11 points at times, but Robey kept the Celtics within reach and Cedric Maxwell demonstrated his ability to shine under pressure. The Celtics started running, and when they called to the bench, in came M.L. Carr and an impossibly young Kevin McHale.

At quarter's end, the Celtics trailed by four, but an easily overlooked thing happened: Bobby Jones missed a buzzer beater, and Robey love-slapped Steve Mix on the way to terra firma. The Celtics swarmed around, and some police sprang into action, but when it counted, only Bobby Jones, Caldwell Jones, and Andrew Toney come to the aid of their teammate.

The Celtics seized the momentum early in the fourth. Parish was back and challenging his opponents and even Bird for rebounds. Erving and Darryl Dawkins were sitting with foul trouble, and Boston regained the lead. Then they lost it again, and with 5:23 left in the game, Dr. J scored to extend the Sixers lead to 89–82.

After that basket the Celtics held Philly to one point, as the Celtics handcuffed the Sixers with steals. The Chief and Maxwell (and McHale in the third) were cleaning the sinuses out of everybody in their way. Later Darryl Dawkins lamented, "What can I say, man? It hurts…it's the worst. It's over, man, and I ain't getting into no trouble. I ain't going to blame the refs, but you run the [bleeping] film back when I took my shot and you tell me if two guys didn't get me. You look at it and tell me. I didn't get a goddamned call…. I got three guys on me, I get knocked down, and there's no call. What kind of [bleep] is that?"

Run the tape back—even without Johnny Most commentating, you'll see the Celtics got mugged at the end of fast breaks, and Caldwell Jones hammered Bird down low after beating out Dr. J. It was tough, but in the crunch Parish made a trademark turnaround jumper, Archibald hit his foul shots, and Bird iced it with a bank shot that harked back to the days of Sam Jones. Run the tape back and try to find Dr. J commanding the game or Andrew Toney anywhere.

The Celtics won 91–90 to advance to the NBA Finals against the Rockets.

Classy Julius Erving, along with three of his teammates and coach Billy Cunningham, visited the Celtics locker room after the game to congratulate them. Approaching Eric Fernsten, Erving simply said, "Nice foul." Outside of the Garden, bedlam reigned, with the Boston police arresting one fan for directing traffic. Allegedly, alcohol was a factor.

Similar to the Phoenix Suns of 1976, the 40–42 Houston Rockets did not belong in the championship series, yet after four games, their series was tied 2–2 with Boston. Game 5 was meant for Cedric Maxwell, and he did everything but make Moses Malone one of the permanent statues along Commonwealth Avenue, leading all scorers with 28 points as he propelled his men to victory. Larry Bird called it "one of the greatest football games I've ever seen Cedric Maxwell play." Of course Boston had some added incentive, because Moses Malone claimed that he and four of his high school teammates could defeat the Celtics.

Boston mercifully ended it on May 14 in Houston, closing out the Rockets 102–91. To the surprise of no one, Bird (27 points) played great, and Robert Parish began to establish his reputation as perhaps the

Red Auerbach should have loved the dedication and intensity that Cedric Maxwell brought to the floor each evening, but instead the two clashed. Long having made peace with his past, Max is now a popular broadcaster for the team.

preeminent center in the NBA, scoring most of his team's points before fouls benched him. But this was Cedric Maxwell's night and his series, chosen MVP and earning the praise of Bill Fitch: "One of the real keys to the game was in the second when the Rockets decided to use Robert Reid to double up on Max, who was hurting them inside. Once Reid did that, it freed up [Larry Bird], who started hitting his outside shot. Maxwell can be that effective both on offense and defense. And when he gets out in the lanes and really runs, there isn't a forward in the league that can stay with him."

One forgotten aspect of this series is that Kevin McHale rarely played, a presence only in the second game when he scored 12 points. That would soon change. In the meantime, Moses Malone, in contrast to Dr J, failed to go down graciously, reiterating, "I'm not changing anything I said."

Boston staged a massive rally at City Hall Plaza, at which time Larry Bird surveyed the crowd and graciously proclaimed, "I look out at this crowd and I see one thing that typifies our season—Moses does eat shit!"

chapter 23

Sixers and Kevins

1981–82

Younger NBA fans do not know who Andrew Toney is, a shame because at this juncture of his career he had promised to develop into one of the greatest guards in league history and a massive Celtics killer in the process. He promised to lead a very talented group of team-mates (Julius Erving, Mo Cheeks, Caldwell Jones, Darryl Dawkins, and Bobby Jones) into dominance, for as Larry Bird once observed, "Do I remember Andrew Toney? The Boston Strangler? Yeah, I remember him. I wish we would've had him. He was a killer. We called him the Boston Strangler because every time he got a hold of the ball we knew he was going to score. He was the absolute best I've ever seen at shooting the ball at crucial times. We had nobody who could come close to stopping him. Nobody."

By the time Charles Barkley joined the team, stress fractures in Toney's feet had ruined his career as Philadelphia descended in the rankings, but while he played, Toney excelled. The rivalry between the Celtics and 76ers had revived, exceeding even the days of Bill Russell versus Wilt Chamberlain, and to keep ahead of the competition, Red Auerbach had to feed the monster with guards, choosing Charles Bradley from Wyoming, Tracy Jackson from Notre Dame early in the second, and then shortly later, Danny Ainge from Brigham Young University.

That's when things got interesting. Harking back to the time when Red had to fight with major league baseball for the services for Gene Conley, the Celtics had to fight hard for the Blue Jays' Danny Ainge. Red had shrewdly drafted the BYU star guard in the second round, correctly discerning that he might want to forsake baseball for basketball. In his third major league season Ainge had batted .187 and sagely decided to play basketball, but Toronto fought.

Blue Jays GM Peter Bavasi went to Auerbach's own playbook and decided to make a fuss over the Celtics wanting to steal his player. But before compensation for Ainge became an issue, the dispute landed in federal court, venued to New York. The Celtics contended that some words of encouragement allegedly said by Bavasi to Ainge, to the effect of "chase your dreams," constituted essentially the Jays' release of Ainge to play basketball. The federal court agreed with the Jays and Red came back from the incident red-faced. Now he either had to forget about the whole matter or pay the Blue Jays suitable compensation.

Shortly after the draft 76ers coach Billy Cunningham was asked about stopping the Celtics, and he deadpanned that he would get lessons to make Ainge a better hitter and thus keep him in Toronto. On a serious note, Auerbach began suspecting as matters progressed that both Philly and L.A. had engaged in tampering, trying to drive up the price the Celtics had to pay for Ainge. Or even better, getting Ainge to sit out a year and sign with their clubs.

One rumor abounded during the Danny Ainge matter: that the Blue Jays, San Diego Padres, and Celtics meant to consummate the first three-team deal involving a basketball club and baseball clubs. The Blue Jays would trade Ainge to San Diego for prospects while Boston rented Danny from the Padres for $300,000 per year. The bizarre transaction never occurred, but after Ainge had joined Boston in early December, a roster move had to take place and someone had to go. To make room for Ainge, the Celtics sold rookie guard Tracy Jackson to the Bulls with Auerbach explaining, "I didn't want to put him on waivers, because then you don't know where he might wind up. So we made a deal, primarily to help the kid." Then again, had Jackson played a mean second base...

Unburdened with the necessity of trying to carry a team, Nate "Tiny" Archibald became a very effective team player after he came to Boston.

Red bit the bitter pill and paid for Ainge's rights. He later made noise about tampering and some talk leaked that the Celtics wanted Philly and L.A.'s first draft choices, but the matter soon died. Having spent the money on Ainge, the club had to endure his growing pains while simultaneously not providing him with enough playing time to mature. It mattered little when they went a league-best 63–19, but it did haunt them in the playoffs.

In the Eastern Conference semis, the Celtics deceptively dispatched with the Washington Bullets in five games. These were the same Bullets who went 43–39 and whose third leading scorer, Spencer Haywood, had won a gold medal with Jo Jo White in 1968 and who was once wed to David Bowie's current wife, Iman. It was also the team of Rick Mahorn and Jeff Ruland, christened by Johnny Most as "McFilthy" and "McNasty," and Boston went into overtime for their third win and into double OT for the fourth and deciding victory against this extraordinarily physical opponent.

Having very literally just fought their way through the hell of the Bullets, the Celtics now faced their rivals, the Sixers, and it got no more hospitable in Philly. After splitting the first two games, the Celtics not only lost Game 3 by two points; they also lost Tiny Archibald, who sustained a dislocated shoulder. Archibald had led the Celtics in points and assists in the previous contest.

Little has been made about the loss of Archibald, certainly not comparable to the injury to John Havlicek in 1973, which probably cost the Celtics a championship then. This time, the Celtics' depth absorbed this loss, and although they lost the third and fourth games, they rallied to win the fifth and six games.

Tiny Archibald was not the only Celtic requiring medical attention in the Sixers series. Danny Ainge needed stitches for his lip, and Rick Robey required some for an elbow injury.

Traditionally, Boston never lost a Game 7. The Celtics had home-court advantage over the Sixers, so instinctively, it looked good for Boston. It simply did not end that way.

Andrew Toney played one of his finest games, and the Celtics committed too many mistakes at critical times. Danny Ainge scored 17 points in only 28 minutes but committed costly turnovers and accumulated five fouls. Kevin McHale scored 20, but he too racked up five fouls and missed two critical free throws. Larry Bird scored 20 points but shot only 7-for-18 from the floor, and Robert Parish experienced a similar phenomenon. Bill Fitch had Bird guarding Toney at some points, a coaching error.

In the last seconds of the game, the heartbroken Garden fans had one last thing to say to the 76ers: "Beat L.A.! Beat L.A.! Beat L.A.!"

Eulogized Larry Bird, "It hurts more than anything. I can't compare it to losing in college, because it is a different situation. Today we fought back and had a lot of challenges and showed our composure. We had a great year. But this is the second season, and we failed."

Of course, they failed no one. There is no shame in losing to a very good team, and the team had excelled in a city that had lost much of its cachet; the Patriots had never won a championship, the Sox had last hoisted a banner in 1918, the Bruins would not win another Stanley Cup until the new millennium, and the Braves had vanished altogether.

This team brought joy to the region and gave its fans innumerable memories and fodder to discuss on the beaches and at the clam shacks all summer long. The clipper ships no longer sailed into the harbor from all coordinates of the globe, and perhaps Boston no longer struck anyone any longer as the Hub of the world. But maybe it could be again.

1982–83

Whether Moses Malone was eating what Larry Bird had suggested two seasons prior was unknown, but whatever he was eating, he was now doing it in Philadelphia. The Sixers had beefed up their roster by adding free agent Malone, who joined Julius Erving, Andrew Toney, Maurice Cheeks, and Bobby Jones to create the finest team in the NBA. Though Boston split its season series with Philly, it finished nine games behind its rivals in the Atlantic Division standings.

If you want Dickensian characters, read *David Copperfield* or *A Christmas Carol*, do not immediately cast Red Auerbach in such a role. In the spring, he drafted Landon Turner, an Indiana University national champion who was paralyzed in a car accident before his senior season, a classic gesture. He also sent Turner NBA championship rings after the Celtics won in 1984 and 1986. Then again, before venerating Red, recall that in 1969, he insisted on a body in exchange for long-retired Bob Cousy, who wanted to serve as a player/coach for the Cincinnati Royals. Something similar happened in 1982–83, as the Bucks wanted long dormant Dave Cowens, and Auerbach squeezed Quinn Buckner out of them in exchange.

Auerbach executed a good deal in January, adding small forward Scott Wedman (a two-time All-Star) while giving up little; Wedman scored off the bench and played particularly well in the playoffs. The arrival of Wedman coincided with a divergence between Nate Archibald and Fitch, with the coach curtailing his point guard's playing time, increasingly preferring Danny Ainge and Quinn Buckner.

Archibald openly called out the coach: "One of the things I noticed off the bench was that we needed direction. But I was on the bench and there was nothing I could do about it." While Fitch increasingly relied on Buckner, Buckner did not seem to appreciate Fitch. Cedric Maxwell had ceased talking to the press, and his offense sagged. Increasingly the players tuned out Fitch, and in the last stretch of the season, his charges compiled a 12–10 record.

Fitch had fallen in love with Larry Bird, pretty understandable being that his star finished in the top 10 league-wide in points, total rebounds, free throw percentage, and minutes played. A first-team All-NBA and a second-team All-Defensive selection, Bird placed second in the voting for MVP. On a less positive note, Fitch continued to treat even mundane regular season games as though he was facing elimination in the Finals, hollering like Captain Ahab and fretting like Captain Queeg. Most players treated his verbosity as annoying background noise: a barking dog or a cranky old man yelling at the neighborhood kids for running across his lawn.

Despite the late-season lapse, the Celtics still sported the third-best overall record in the NBA and defeated the Hawks in the first round of the playoffs. Then they let the Bucks, led by their coach and erstwhile Celtic Don Nelson, sweep them. Just like that, it was over. Guillotine season had arrived early.

Some Celtics fanatics believe that Danny Ainge bit Tree Rollins of the Hawks in the playoff clincher, undoubtedly due in part to the guard's reputation for feistiness on the court. Their fight started when Rollins was transitioning to defense and threw an elbow into Ainge's face. Danny responded by tackling Tree. A pileup ensued, but camerawork clearly showed Rollins treating Ainge's finger as a Buffalo wing. Danny required five stitches and contemplated suing while Rollins had to endure headlines like "Tree's Bite Is Worse Than His Bark." Speaking of lawsuits, Rollins had recently dropped his own against M.L. Carr for $1 million for allegedly pulling a knife on him after a game.

It started with Bill Fitch, who received a vote of confidence, but then he quit after owner Harry Mangurian decided he no longer wanted to own a team. Who really knows? By this time the players largely had stopped listening to Fitch, so whether he quit, got fired, or lost himself in the Arnold Arboretum, he left to coach the Houston Rockets.

Tellingly, when the Celtics hired a new coach, they chose K.C. Jones, an assistant coach who knew the players and how they wanted to be coached, understood the area's fans (having played in the Hub), and had a few ideas of his own about how to restore a championship atmosphere. For example, he perceived how teams collapsed their defenses on the big three of Bird, Parish, and McHale, so he needed to develop or obtain some outside shooting. K.C. did not simply roll the ball out on the floor and let the players play.

Contrasting the different coaching philosophies of Bill Fitch and K.C. Jones, Danny Ainge distilled it this way: "K.C. just makes it fun to play. There's enough pressure out there without having to face more pressure knowing the coach is going to yank you out and yell at you if you make a mistake. At this stage of the game everybody knows when they screw up." Ainge never forgot the lesson in his later incarnation as general manager, hiring Doc Rivers as coach.

But an opposing defense might not even have those worries, as it appeared unlikely the team could resign Kevin McHale, a free agent who had all but changed his area code to sign with the Knicks in New York. This is where having Red Auerbach on one's side pays off. In one of the shrewdest schemes in sports history, Red signed three Knicks—Rory Sparrow, Sly Williams, and Marvin Webster—to offer sheets.

The Knicks fell for the ruse and matched the offers and then found themselves stuck when no suckers wanted to trade one of their stars for Sparrow and Webster (Alex English was mentioned in rumors). Caught in cap hell, the Knicks thereupon passed on McHale, and Boston signed him to a lucrative contract. Of course, now the team had to worry about signing Bird, with one year left on his contract, plus Parish wanted to renegotiate.

In the past, a shrewd roster move or two generally brought the Celtics back a title. In this case, Rick Robey was traded to Phoenix, seemingly because he provided too effective a party pal for young, impressionable Larry Bird. In fact, by this time the only two NBA players capable of stopping Larry Bird were Magic Johnson and Rick Robey. Whatever the root of this trade, after the draft choices back and forth were ironed out, Boston received point guard Dennis Johnson, an unbelievable return in value. Bird, like Prince Hal, had lost his Falstaff, and Parish lacked a backup.

Then they waived Tiny Archibald, eliminating a man who failed to notice that the lights had changed and that starting no longer suited him, though he did have a role to play as a useful substitution. Instead he became bitter and a drag on the team, so off he went.

Off too went Harry Mangurian, who had his sale to the triumvirate of Alan Cohen, Don F. Gaston, and Paul DuPee approved by the league. The finest owner since Walter Brown, Mangurian cleaned up the John Y. debris, brought a title to Boston, and hung around long enough to ensure future prosperity. Like Walter Brown, a nice man, Harry Mangurian gave the fans the 1980s.

chapter 24

K.C. Brings a Banner to Boston

1983–84

A great regular season from start (winning nine out of 10) to finish (winning 10 of the final 11, with the one loss suffered in OT), the Celtics under new coach K.C. Jones finished 62–20, nearly 100 percentage points higher than any other NBA club.

Dennis Johnson, an *enfant terrible* with his previous teams, became a future Hall of Famer in Boston; he toned down his partying and clubhouse lawyering, helping offensively while earning second-team All-Defensive honors. Larry Bird earned his first MVP Award, as he too was selected second-team All-Defensive, while he finished first league-wide in free throw percentage and top 10 in rebounds and minutes played per game.

Rather than sulking over contract negotiations, sixth man Kevin McHale had his highest points total to date, while Robert Parish rebounded magnificently on both sides of the court while scoring more than 1,500 points. With the addition of Johnson and the continued effective play of Gerald Henderson, Danny Ainge lost minutes, Cedric Maxwell maximized his chances to spell Bird or McHale, and rookie Greg Kite filled in for Parish.

In the first round of the playoffs, Boston dispatched with the Bullets in four, despite some very tough opposing play by Jeff Ruland and Rick Mahorn. Tenderized, the Celtics nearly lost the next series to Bernard King and the Nets, until Bird sealed the seventh and deciding game in the

Garden with 39 points. In the Eastern Conference Finals, Boston turned the tables on the previous year's nemesis, nearly sweeping the Bucks, with solid offensive contributions from everyone burying Milwaukee.

Larry Bird had another opportunity to face Magic Johnson in the NBA Finals, but the focus shifted game to game, no surprise in a series with nine future Hall of Famers on the floor. With all of those stars in the firmament, a man who never played in one All-Star contest, Cedric Maxwell, schooled all.

Game 1: the Lakers stole the first game at the Garden 115–109, running the Celtics silly in the first quarter. No half-court team, the Lakers boomeranged the old Celtics fast break against Boston as Kareem Abdul-Jabbar, Magic Johnson, and James Worthy blew Boston off the floor. No nuance here—L.A. swarmed McHale, Bird, and Parish down low and dared Boston to beat them with its guards.

Game 2: some clown kept pulling the fire alarm in the middle of the night at the Lakers' hotel, keeping the mellow Californians on constant edge. Calling Mr. Auerbach? L.A. fans maintain that the Lakers gave this game away, but although Bird led his team in points and rebounds, it was unsung heroes Danny Ainge and Scott Wedman who shot out the lights in this three-point Celtics victory. Pat Riley had dared Boston to win from the perimeter, and for now, he had lost his gambit.

The game went into overtime, and Max closed the deal for his team. Conceded Pat Riley after the game, "He's a great opportunistic player. Those offensive rebounds really killed us. Maybe we didn't cover him as much as we should or as much as we will from now on…. Bird and McHale and Parish get a lot of the media, but Cedric is the glue that brings it all together."

Steve Krischel, a massage therapist friend of Scott Wedman's, entered Celtics lore briefly when he worked on Robert Parish's sore left shoulder, indicating to at least one writer that Robert probably should not be playing. Soon after, assistant general manager Jan Volk barred Krischel from the locker room.

Game 3: Lakers 137, Celtics 104. Tommy Heinsohn questioned D.J.'s Celtichood, and others wondered if Robert Parish had already started his summer vacation. Celtics fans from Presque Isle, Maine, to Rockfall, Connecticut, threw their empty (and a few full) beer cans at their television screens. After the deluge, Larry Bird said the Celtics had played like "sissies."

Game 4: embarrassed, Boston got nasty. Rebounding a missed jumper, Kareem heaved the ball down the floor to Worthy, who tossed it to Kurt Rambis on what should be an easy basket, making the Celtics look like the Washington Generals. Instead, Kevin McHale mugged Rambis, heaving him to the floor. Now *that's* a foul! Bob Brannum, Dave Cowens, and Jim Loscutoff could not have done it any better. Pat Riley called the Celtics "thugs." Rambis enjoyed the finest of revenges, being possibly the only American male in history to look appreciably more handsome in his fifties than he did in his twenties.

At that time the Lakers led by six points, but by the end of the third, Boston trailed by only two. The Celtics won it in L.A. in OT 129–125. McHale got points for the takedown, but Bird, Parish, and D.J. accounted for most of the offensive punch.

When told of Riley's comments, Red Auerbach said, "He is just saying that 'cause he got beat."

A rough series, Scott Wedman sustained a leg injury that knocked him out of the game and into a wheelchair for the flight back to Logan Airport.

Game 5: in the heat of the Garden, Bird led his Celtics to a comfortable win with 34 points and 17 rebounds, breaking from a recent mini-slump. As Pat Riley conceded, "The man who made the difference was Bird. He was just awesome. He made everything work. He was the catalyst, and that's what happens when great players come to the front." Jabbar and Magic could not hit their shots, and Boston breezed in the final 24 minutes. The Bermuda Air Mass caused a ref to leave the game due to dehydration.

Game 6: the Lakers came out fighting, literally, with James Worthy shoving Cedric Maxwell in the back and threatening to take a swing at Danny Ainge. Just settling accounts, claimed Worthy: "They do it to us—they've got to expect something back. They've been verbally abusing us, and Maxwell made the choke sign. That's not professional." Pat Riley seconded the roughhousing: "I don't think what he did to Max was anything near what McHale did to Kurt. Worthy didn't grab him around the neck and throw him to the floor."

A Lakers' 36–12 run killed the Celtics.

Think that the David Stern bashing started with disgraced ref Tim Donaghy? A little birdie had whispered into Larry Bird's ear that Stern really, really wanted a Game 7 in this series. Said Bird, "When Stern makes a statement like that, things are going to happen." These accusations are as old as the sport; old-timers recall former commissioner Walter Kennedy taking trips to the referee's bathroom during the half rather than using his much nicer commish's plumbing. Back in 1890s Springfield, someone probably once accused James Naismith of lowering the peach baskets for one team to the detriment of the other.

Game 7: with the passing of each year, the heat that the teams played in at the Garden on this night only goes up in the memories of those present—or those who say they were there. The highest estimate is 97 degrees, but someday someone will swear it rose about 100, with Red Auerbach allegedly flipping the switch himself. Certainly a fast-breaking club flourished better with air conditioning, but who cares? No one was going to defeat Cedric Maxwell this evening, as he reassured his teammates: "Well boys, one more time. Just hop on my back and I'll take you on it."

As a team the Lakers shot considerably better than Boston, but except for Kareem, all of their starters and some of their reserves labored with foul problems. In the end, that telling trend cost L.A. the title. The Celtics scored 43 points on free throws while the Lakers had only 28 opportunities from the stripe and made only 18.

But no one who saw the game at the Garden or on the family couch broke that down, neither did they hear Cedric Maxwell taunting James Worthy, reminding the former Tar Heel, "You can't guard me!" Bird, Parish, and D.J. did not shoot well from the floor, but Max did, scoring

17 of his points in the first half. Boston let the saunalike conditions in the final 24 sap the strength from L.A. and their fast-breaking ways and won 111–102. Pat Riley had said a lot during the series; now M.L. Carr had a few words of advice for the Lakers coach: "He should just sit on the bench with his pretty suit and ugly face and just coach."

Never an All-Star, Cedric Maxwell played his best against L.A., although Bird was named the series MVP.

NBA champions!

1984–85

A typically excellent year—63–19, Atlantic Division champions—but ultimately a disappointing one, as the team fell to the Lakers in the NBA Finals in six games. Boston had progressed so much as a franchise that simply playing in the Finals constituted no honor; only winning the last game of the playoffs did.

To extend the excellence, the club picked up free agent point guard Ray Williams from the Knicks, having to relinquish only two second-round draft choices, and though no longer a star, Williams scored 6.4 points per game and played well early as soon as the playoffs commenced. Nice pickup.

In a November game against the Sixers, Larry Bird lit up the floor while Julius Erving delivered bricks all day in a game the Celtics eventually won. But before that happened, both stars were ejected for fighting, Bird probably being most responsible not only for embarrassing Dr. J but by sending elbows at him for punctuation. Moses Malone and Charles Barkley wrapped up Bird while Erving threw some punches at his tormentor. Only Celts assistant Chris Ford got bloodied, trying to intercede to end the violence. Cedric Maxwell surveyed the massacre in deadpan fashion, philosophizing, "It was no big deal. Neither one of 'em could bust a grapefruit."

In February, Maxwell underwent a relatively minor arthroscopic surgery on his knee and did not return to the lineup for way too long a

For too many years, Dennis Johnson was denied entrance into the Hall of Fame, an honor that was bestowed upon him posthumously. Celtics fans knew what they had, and Larry Bird considered Johnson his finest teammate.

period to assuage Red Auerbach, who had supposedly retired as GM. In his stead, McHale became an acknowledged NBA star, no longer a sixth man, though ironically he won the Sixth Man of the Year Award that season. He defended well, blocked shots, and fooled everybody offensively down low. He scored the most points ever in a game by a Celtic with 56 on March 3 against the Pistons. Of course, Larry Bird broke the record with 60 points against the Hawks in New Orleans nine days later, with most fans left wondering why it took him that long.

Bemusedly watching this was star center Robert Parish, accumulating another fine campaign at 17.6 points and 10.6 rebounds per game. Larry Bird did not often compliment McHale, but he raved about Dennis Johnson: "He makes so many things happen at both ends of the court. He can penetrate. And people say he's not a great shooter, but he shoots about 47 percent, and that's all right. Defensively, he is one of the best. He can play people tight, and he can anticipate very well. And he's always ready to play when it matters."

Sick of hearing about Larry Bird already? Tough; to borrow an Auerbach line, people already forget how great he really was. A repeat MVP, he scored 28.7 points per game, led the league in minutes played per game, and finished in the top 10 for rebounds per game. He led the team in steals and trailed only playmaking guard Dennis Johnson in assists (543 to 531). Impressive, but like analyzing the play of Bill Russell, the statistics only superficially describe his game. He made incredible passes, played peerless defense, chased loose balls, and performed even better during clutch moments.

Boston breezed through the first three rounds of the playoffs, losing only four games, for the privilege of vying again for the championship with Los Angeles. Pushed around the previous year, Pat Riley had his charges bashing the Celtics all series, causing K.C. Jones to complain about the rough play. Thugs.

In 1983–84, the Garden was too hot, but this time the Celtics' shooting was too cold, particularly D.J., Ainge, and Bird. D.J. did ice a victory with his buzzer beater in the fourth game to tie the series, but this time they largely played without Max; Scott Wedman formed a de facto one-man bench with Ray Williams also ailing.

The errant shooting destroyed Boston, with only Kevin McHale (32 points, .611 shooting percentage) proving effective as Bird shot .414 and Parish went 5-for-14, D.J. 3-for-15, and Ainge 3-for-16, in the sixth and deciding game at the Garden.

Did an altercation at an off–Quincy Market bar cost the Celtics another championship? On May 16, 1985, Larry Bird, Quinn Buckner, and another friend were allegedly at Chelsea's, a long-defunct Boston saloon. An altercation erupted, spilling out to the street, with Bird possibly injuring his right thumb. Don't look to Chelsea's—it's no longer there. Finger the Celtics bench or lack thereof; when the Lakers relied on reserves such as Michael Cooper, Mitch Kupchak, and a resurrected Bob McAdoo in the NBA Finals, K.C. Jones had little left with the exception of sharp shooting Scott Wedman to call on.

As good as the Celtics were, to defeat the Lakers, some bodies had to go, as Quinn Buckner and one of the team's superstars had played their last games in Boston. About Cedric Maxwell, Auerbach bluntly stated, "Needless to say, I was a little disappointed in his rehabilitation. I just don't know what we're gonna do with him—or anybody else."

The Celtics had not been swept in the Finals, but the brooms had come out anyway.

chapter 25
'86

1985–86

If you had Celtics seasons tickets in 1985–86, you saw your favorite team lose only once. This is the club that went 40–1 at home, even though three of the home games were at the Hartford Civic Center. Everything seemed to go right in 1986: the economy boomed with the Massachusetts Miracle that almost propelled governor Michael Dukakis to the White House; the Red Sox came within one pitch of their first World Series victory since the year that Ted Williams was born; Sam and Diane still loved each other on *Cheers*; and people still had minor surgery done at St. Elsewhere Hospital. Boston was the Hub of the world.

Five of the team's top six players eventually earned induction into the Basketball Hall of Fame: center Robert Parish, forwards Larry Bird and Kevin McHale, and guard Dennis Johnson, plus a newcomer, eventual Sixth Man of the Year Award–winner Bill Walton. Do not forget the other starting guard, Danny Ainge, who knocked down more than half his shots from the floor and over 90 percent from the line. His three-point shooting also improved by almost 100 percent in one year, as he played very consistent basketball, dispelling much of the criticism of his game from previous years.

Obtaining their new sixth man did not come free or easy, as a simmering feud between Red Auerbach and Cedric Maxwell greased Max's ride out of town. On September 6, Boston traded its forward along with a first-round pick (used for future Hall of Famer Arvydas Sabonis) to the Clippers for Bill Walton. Finally healthy, in limited time Walton scored more than 600 points and blocked more than 100 shots, and fans who

Though his time with the Celtics was brief, Bill Walton joined Kevin McHale, Larry Bird, and Robert Parish in one of NBA history's most formidable front lines.

once from afar viewed him as a dangerous hippie now saw him as a red-headed Irish guy, quite literally a Celt.

Although he played only a little more than one season in Boston, he is forever thought of as a Celtic, personifying the traits traditionally associated with the franchise's championship players: intelligence, hard work, ability to function at a high level with his teammates, and an appreciation of what it takes to win. Plus, he lightened the mood by loving the Grateful Dead and wearing a Nixon mask to practice one Halloween.

Gospel has it that Cedric Maxwell simply disappeared after he shipped out to the Clippers. Not so—in 1985–86, he scored 14.1 points per game and compiled his third-highest number of rebounds. Never known as a scorer, Cedric Maxwell possesses the greatest true shooting percentage in the history of the NBA.

Superlatives aside, Walton accepted a role as Robert Parish's backup at center, scoring 7.6 points per game but more important, still rebounding and blocking shots at a superb level. For the first time in his career, he played in nearly every game, a defender who ceaselessly devised ways to shut out opposing shooters and then seamlessly executed these schemes with his teammates. Despite making this remarkably successful trade, Auerbach had not finished dealing.

An October trade brought point guard Jerry Sichting from the Pacers for two second-round draft choices, and this short and scrawny point guard not only gave Dennis Johnson needed rest, but he also presented one of the more unique scoring profiles in NBA history. Sichting scored 6.5 points per game, but had he played more and shot more, his numbers at free throw percentage, field goal percentage, and three-point percentage, when projected out, reside at the top 10 in the NBA in all these categories.

Sichting obviously presented a less-is-more résumé, because he generally never shot anywhere near as well when playing more minutes, firing away on inferior teams when opposing defenders were not swarming his superstar teammates. Yet in his role as a backup guard, he excelled. Plus, like Ainge, he got on the nerves of his opponents, just another element of harassment unleashed on a strong defense.

The lone Celtics home loss occurred on December 6, 1985, in a game against the Portland Trail Blazers. After the 18-point drubbing, mischievous media members tried to egg on Mychal Thompson to diss Boston, causing the Blazers center/forward to diplomatically counter, "My few rules in life are these: you don't cheat on the IRS; you don't curse the Lord; and you don't get Larry Bird mad. So let's just say they had a flat night."

After this team lost Ray Williams, it signed Sly Williams. After Sly Williams' hemorrhoids kept him off the floor, Auerbach signed up David Thirdkill. With Scott Wedman splitting most of the minutes off the bench with Walton and Sichting, other reserves such as Greg Kite, Sam Vincent, and Rick Carlisle saw little action until after a slow patch around Yuletime, when K.C. rested the starters more.

These players were so much fun to watch. Fans witnessed Bird winning his third straight MVP Award, McHale becoming a superstar, Parish owning opponents on defense and becoming a more skilled passer, Dennis Johnson shutting down the best opposing player on defense, a confident Danny Ainge knocking down shots from the three-point line and beyond, and Bill Walton, the former Portland center who carried that franchise to a title years before only to have injuries muck up his career, turning to Boston to demonstrate his greatness and a selfless devotion to team plays.

One of the few criticisms about this roster was the fact that two-thirds of the players were Caucasian in a league predominantly African American. Had the Celtics organization, which drafted the first African American collegian, started five African American players before anyone else, and hired the first African American coach suddenly succumbed to racism? Maybe not consciously, but some of the Celtics' draft choices and acquisitions in this era brought in white players that even Bailey Howell might have considered too straight-laced. And they could not play NBA basketball.

Even when this team lost, as it did in early January against Bill Laimbeer and the Pistons, it never failed to entertain. The roughhousing began when Parish took a swing at Laimbeer and Isiah Thomas incurred a technical for throwing a ball at the Celtics center. "We don't like Laimbeer too good," summed up Larry Bird. After the game ended, normally mild-mannered K.C. Jones accosted a ref, loudly inquiring, "What the [bleep] are you doing in this league?"

By this time the phrase "triple double" had entered the lexicon of Celtics Nation, as Larry Bird perfected the art, the only player on the roster, in fact, who had ever accomplished the feat. Perhaps back in the day Bob Cousy did it, but incomplete record keeping made it impossible to determine.

Most Celtics fanatics know that their team went 40–1 at home this year, but almost no one appreciates that this team went on a 29-game streak where it pulled down more rebounds than its opponents.

Even K.C. Jones knew enough to provide this team an occasional break. At the beginning of a late-season practice at Hellenic College, the coach told the team that if one player could hit a shot from center court, he would cancel the practice. Naturally, Larry Bird got a ball, set himself up at half-court, and arced the ball in, all net. Practice canceled. The team had nothing else to work on other than prepare for the playoffs, with the first-round opponent Michael Jordan's Chicago Bulls.

Tough Boston swept the Bulls, although Jordan nearly willed his team past the Celtics. In the second game, he scored 63 points, after which Larry Bird anointed his foe the greatest player who ever lived. The Celtics had seen the future and survived, with Danny Ainge having a particularly fine series, causing K.C. Jones to note, "He's driving to the basket. He has that look in his eye, like he's playing the total game—which he is. His defense has really impressed me this year."

Against Dominique Wilkins and the Hawks in the Eastern Conference semifinals, Boston prevailed in five, in the final contest outscoring Atlanta 36–6 in the third quarter.

Long before he became the Celtics coach, Doc Rivers, as an Atlanta Hawks guard, impressed everyone from Boston with his poise. Never a man to get testy when posed a tough question or to fail to provide an intelligent and thoughtful answer, he also won over the Massachusetts media with his wit. When asked about his upcoming nuptials, he intimated that the men in his wedding party had chosen black sneakers to wear (a foreshadowing of his later Celtics tenure?) and he had already picked out pink basketball shoes, "To match my fiancée's dress."

In the Eastern Conference Finals, the Celtics swept Don Nelson's Bucks, with the only controversy concocted by a Milwaukee barrister who saw Robert Parish and Larry Bird sniffing from a capsule during the game. A federal case was made until it transpired that these were ammonia capsules and nothing else, causing Bird to deadpan, "Anytime the Celtics want me to take a urinalysis, I'll do it any time, any place. It's just sickening. I've never been involved in anything like that. All I do is drink beer, and that gets me in enough trouble."

That left coach Bill Fitch and his Houston Rockets, mostly propelled by their Twin Towers, the estimable Hakeem Olajuwon and Ralph Sampson. Dennis Johnson led the Celtics in rebounds, as did Robert Parish in points scored and Larry Bird in assists. They demonstrated that every team member could perform astonishing feats as the Celtics won the first game. They took the second contest in the heat of the Garden, during which Bird scored 31 points accompanied by eight rebounds and seven assists, causing Fitch to observe, "When he gets in that rhythm, there isn't anyone who can stop him. I thought we stopped him in the third quarter, but then he got into one of his 'playing in his own back-yard' situations where he is in his own world and it seems like he's out there alone. When he gets going like that, he is awesome." So was Kevin McHale in the low post, contributing 25 points.

The Celtics blew a lead in the fourth period to lose the third game 106–104, but McHale preserved a victory in the fourth game with a timely late steal. It is the next game, however, that everyone remembers or has since learned about on Grandpa's knee.

In Houston, down 3–1 in the series, Ralph Sampson and the Rockets were mad as hell, culminating in Ralph Tin Tin fighting diminutive guard Jerry Sichting. Sichting gamely returned the salvo, staying alive until reinforcements, then Dennis Johnson and Bill Walton, attacked Sampson. Olajuwon joined in, cutting D.J. above the left eye, energizing the roughhousing Rockets and forcing a sixth game back at the Garden. Dispensing a kindly bit of advice for Ralph Sampson, Bird mused, "I think Ralph will have a tough time in Boston. He better wear his hard hat."

Yes, Johnny Most was terrific on the air, apoplectically analyzing the great Sampson/Sichting boxing match: "Sampson levels Sichting with an elbow; now they're fighting.... They don't call it. He started the whole damn thing. And big Ralph Sampson is a foot and three inches taller than Sichting...he's the last guy who has a right to complain. The big, brave bull. 'I'm Ralph Sampson. I have the right to hit you. I have a right to bite your head off.' Ralph Sampson is a gutless big guy who picks on little people, and he showed me a gutless streak. That was a gutless, yellow thing to do." Damn, we miss Johnny Most!

The problem for Sampson and the Rockets was they had just played their last home game and had to fly to Boston and win both games for the title—the same Garden where the Celtics had not lost a game in nearly six months. They would not do it. Boston fans went after Sampson all afternoon, and Ralph's hooks couldn't catch a thing. A true champion, Larry Bird triple-doubled his mates to a 114–97 victory and another title, with Bird taking one last shot at defeated foe Sampson: "I can't believe he picked a fight with Sichting. Heck, my girlfriend could beat him up."

Kevin McHale had the last words on this memorable season: "Total euphoria."

chapter 26

Accursed Len Bias

1986–87

Len Bias, the greatest Celtic who never was. Before Boston chose him with the second pick of the NBA draft on June 17, 1986, his mother, Lonise, began experiencing fearful premonitions regarding her son, later relating, "I can remember speaking to this woman once before Len died, and she had said, 'Things are going to be so wonderful for you all.' And I remember telling her this very clearly. I said, 'It looks like I can go over to that table and pick up whatever's on that table. It *looks* like I can do it, but there can be something that can stop me from doing it.' So I guess what I'm saying is, while everyone else was cheering, I was still waiting to see if it was going to happen, because…"

Her dread proved all too prescient, as her son overdosed on cocaine as soon as he arrived home in Maryland, having earlier flown to Boston to meet with the team management, the press, and the brass at Reebok, where he inked a $3 million endorsement contract.

Watch videos of this young man playing basketball—do not simply treat him as the flawed hero in a precautionary tale. Often favorably compared with Michael Jordan, Bias outleapt everyone and blocked shots, but he also carried the swagger of a Kevin Garnett and the creativity in shooting and the adapting to his defender of a Larry Bird. A second-team consensus All-American in his junior season at Maryland, he earned first-team consensus honors his senior year as he improved in most categories of his game. He was more than prepared to become an NBA superstar, but was chosen *second* in the NBA draft, after center Brad Daugherty.

Nothing against Brad Daugherty, a center who excelled at North Carolina and played in five All-Star Games as a professional, but Bias was significantly more talented. Rhetorically speaking, why would anyone pick Brad Daugherty over someone with the potential to be one of the 10 greatest basketball players of all time? It made no sense from a fantasy standpoint.

A born-again Christian, Bias did not fool everybody, and yet, when he came up to Boston, he was the soda pop kid. Maybe his high school coach said it best: "If you put him with a bunch of bums, he'd be the best bum. Put him in with good people, and he'd be the best there, too."

Red Auerbach heard none of these rumblings, just raves from folks such as Terrapins coach Lefty Driesell about what a great kid Bias was, an observation that Red himself made at various camps young Len attended. Bias' death was a tragedy, and with considerable time having passed, I hope even Celtics fans more rabid than this author can now see his passing as not a missed opportunity for more banners on the Garden rafters but as a terrible waste of a young life. Had he made better choices, Len Bias would have been 50 years old in 2013.

Bad luck continued to confound this team. Bill Walton, the defending NBA Sixth Man of the Year, played only 112 minutes the entire season, as his right ankle sidelined him. Sharpshooting Scott Wedman did not make it that far, serving only 78 minutes, suffering from a left heel injury that a June operation did not fully mend. Jerry Sichting still played well, but the contributions of the Celtics reserves, the "Green Team," fell far short of their previous edition.

Auerbach tried to fill gaps, introducing forward/center Fred Roberts, former UCLA star Darren Daye, and in a series of 10-day contracts, Conner Henry, but they did not come close to bridging the difference after Walton and Wedman fell. Coupled with no rookies and a growing realization that Sam Vincent would never star at guard, K.C. Jones kept his starters in longer than normal; Kevin McHale and Robert Parish exceeded their total minutes from the previous year by more than 600 and 400, respectively.

Finding fun Fred Roberts stories is like trying to locate the Lost Dutchman gold mine, but interestingly, the draft choice that Boston swapped to obtain Roberts was used to draft none other than Providence's Billy Donovan, now head coach at Florida. Other than that, I got nothing.

Then the starters missed time due to injuries, with Bird's bad back aggravating him and Danny Ainge's ankle causing him to miss some games. Bird and McHale respectively scored 28.1 and 26.1 points per game this season, and when Ainge returned to action he scored 24 points with 11 rebounds and eight assists. But the bench had thinned and K.C. did not particularly trust it.

Boston waived popular reserve forward David Thirdkill two days before Christmas, leaving K.C. Jones to lament, "It's a bad day. Dennis [Johnson] is out with the flu, and we waived David this morning. I look at it that it's very difficult to waive someone who's having a career. He had a very good attitude and he worked hard. It's just the business part of basketball—the cold part."

In the playoffs, Boston dispatched with the Bulls early, even though McHale sat out the third game with a bum ankle. It took seven games to wheeze past a tough Milwaukee Bucks team, but the most memorable games this season came in the Eastern Conference Finals against the Detroit Pistons.

Game 5 is the gem. With five seconds left and the Pistons in possession of the ball, all Isiah Thomas had to do was inbound it successfully and force Boston to foul. Pistons coach Chuck Daly was screaming to call a timeout and Dennis Rodman remembered, "I thought, 'Timeout.' I turned and was coming back to half-court." Instead, Isiah lobbed a pass toward Bill Laimbeer; Bird raced off his defender, stole it, and then fed it to D.J. for the game winner. The Celtics won 108–107.

But that moment barely surpasses the takedown of Bill Laimbeer by Robert Parish earlier in the game. Fed up with Laimbeer, Parish went after the Detroit stalwart as if he were chopping down a tree and miraculously did not get called for a foul, although he was suspended for the next game. It worked out; Parish was injured at the end of Game 5 and may not have suited up for the next one anyway. Everyone in Boston hated Laimbeer, who "knew somebody was going to take a swing at me after K.C. Jones didn't get fined for taking a swing at me in Detroit." Light heavyweight champion Thomas Hearns attended the game and positively critiqued Parish's technique.

Without Parish, Boston lost the sixth tilt but won it all back in the Garden 117–114, causing sour grapes to emit from Dennis Rodman and then Isiah Thomas, who stated, "I think Larry Bird is a very, very good basketball player, an exceptional talent, but I have to agree with Rodman. If he were black, he'd be just another good guy..."

Bird bailed out Thomas, but by this point Isiah had begun to pinch a lot of people's nerves, a major reason why he did not participate in the Olympics on the Dream Team years later.

So much happened in this series that virtually no one remembers that in the seventh game, Detroit's future Hall of Famer Adrian Dantley collided with teammate Vinnie Johnson and had to be transported off the parquet in a stretcher straight to Massachusetts General Hospital with a concussion. At that juncture, Dantley had scored 18 points and had guarded Larry Bird well, and after the former Notre Dame star was carted off, Dennis Rodman frankly did not cut the mustard against Larry Legend, who, after all, was just another good guy.

Boston came into the championship series as underdogs, and the Lakers won in six. Critically, in Game 4 at the Garden, a one-point loss destroyed the Celtics. Their starters outperformed the Lakers starters, but their reserves did very little. L.A.'s Michael Cooper, Mychal Thompson, and Kurt Rambis combined for 26 points, 13 rebounds, and seven assists, while the Boston trio of Greg Kite, Jerry Sichting, and Darren Daye contributed totals of four, two, and one. McHale played with a bad foot throughout, but even most Celtics fans had to concede that L.A. had the better team.

It constituted a reversal from those great Auerbach-coached clubs that had rested Bob Cousy and Bill Sharman and unleashed Sam Jones and K.C. Jones on the opposition. This time L.A. had the depth and Boston had the best starting five. And this year, Magic Johnson, not Larry Bird, won league MVP honors.

1987–88

This was a snake-bit year, starting with an off-the-court lawsuit in which the Celtics fought relocating 33 season ticket holders to install handi-capped seating. They lost and looked insensitive to boot. Meanwhile, Kevin McHale had off-season surgery to repair the broken foot he had played with the previous last season, so he did not suit up until after the first frost.

After enduring disappointing drafts for nearly a decade, the Celtics har-vested a sleeper pick named Reggie Lewis from Northeastern University, a gentle spirit but a tough competitor who played an NCAA tourna-ment game with a broken wrist his junior year. The Celtics thought they had another steal with their second-round draft choice, forward Brad Lohaus from Iowa, and in a sense they did, because even though the draft still prattled on for several rounds, getting any player after the first round helped. Unfortunately, some grossly misinformed people started to compare him to Larry Bird, a horrible weight to put on a young man who ended up having a long NBA career, just not a stellar one.

Robert Parish aged like fine wine, but the other four starters battled injuries at various times after the real games started, and the bench did not always respond. Fred Roberts played very well for bits and pieces, never stitching together a consistent body of work, rendering himself one of the historically least popular Celtics. Artis Gilmore ended his Hall of Fame career in green, and although he did not erase memories of past pickups such as Willie Naulls or Wayne Embry, he did earn player of the game honors once, even though he could barely crawl across the floor.

Most fans at least still considered the Celtics championship contend-ers, and they did finish second overall to the Lakers in total wins (they won another Atlantic Division crown, a dubious achievement because all of their competitors posted losing records). Yet now the Celtics lost more games at home and struggled on the road against even mediocre competition.

It mattered little when they brushed aside the Knicks in the first playoff round, but against the Hawks in the Eastern Conference semis, the Celtics struggled to win in seven. In the last game, fortunately at the Garden, Boston squeaked by 118–116 as Dominique Wilkins and Larry Bird staged one of the most memorable *mano a mano* battles in NBA history; Nique scored 47, one of the highest totals against a Celtics team in playoff history, and Bird snuck in 34 past him, but it was Kevin McHale with 33 points (13-for-13 from the foul line) who deserves as much credit for advancing his team to the next round against Detroit.

Future Celtic Dominique Wilkins had one of his best games ever in the epic seventh game of the semis, admitting, "It's a game I'll remember for a long time. I was just trying to keep the tempo up, and it turned into a shootout. It just seesawed back and forth. It was a hell of a game, and it could have gone either way. We did everything we could, and it came down to who was going to execute in the last two minutes."

And that's where it ended as the Pistons won the series in six games. The Celtics starters outplayed Isiah Thomas and his cohorts, but Chuck Daly used a deep and talented bench (Dennis Rodman, Vinnie Johnson, John Salley, and James Edwards) to wear down Boston. Most of the games were close, all decided by nine points or less, but Detroit had a great defense and Danny Ainge, D.J., and Jim Paxson all labored with bad backs that stifled their shooting as the series progressed.

In the sixth minute of the sixth game, the indomitable Robert Parish left due to a serious bruise to the knee, and Brad Lohaus was tossed for fighting with Dennis Rodman as the Celts went down. Only McHale shot well, despite being mugged after Parish left. Eulogized Danny Ainge, "You have to give them credit. They're the Pistons—and I don't like the Pistons, just don't like 'em—but you have to give them credit."

At the time, it was reported that some Celtics players apparently conceded that Detroit was the better team, and maybe they did. Or maybe if K.C. had fully appreciated the wear and tear placed on his starters by the stringent Detroit defense, he might have used Reggie Lewis more, particularly after the rookie had distinguished himself in the Atlanta series. What is certain is that almost as soon as K.C. Jones alighted from the plane back in Boston, he announced his retirement as coach, with peppery assistant Jimmy Rodgers succeeding him. Things had just gotten a lot more interesting.

chapter 27

After K.C., the Deluge

1988–89

Larry Bird's desire to sort out his contract concerns dominated the off-season, but after this issue smoothed out, the team enjoyed a trip to Spain to participate in the Second McDonald's Basketball Open, where it defeated Real Madrid for the crown. One reporter foolishly asked Bird about the relative merits of American and European basketball, at which point the Hick from French Lick quickly replied, "What do you think?"

What Larry, and soon all of Celtics Nation knew, was that Bird suffered from a pair of sore feet, which he iced frequently; he played for first six games and then never returned, having to undergo surgery at New England Baptist Hospital. Periodically, he tried to return, but that proved impractical. Given the poor state of his team's prospects, extraordinarily unwise.

Bird had been quoted earlier saying, "Teams like Los Angeles, Detroit, and Atlanta all had great benches, and last year, our bench was our downfall. But I think we're making strides this year." Without Bird, they would need a great bench, but early on, their coach had become unruffled, too.

A contrast in styles with K.C. Jones, Jimmy Rodgers blew up at Danny Ainge in one game, labeling him "the stupidest player on the team." On this occasion, the team responded and held its lead, but it continued to play .500 basketball. Far from the "stupidest" player on the team, Ainge had agreed to come off the bench to provide scoring spark for the team, but no change in strategy adequately addressed the absence of Bird, who spent the entire season gamely trying to rehab in time for the playoffs.

In the spirit of improving team chemistry, the Celtics swapped Ainge and inconsistent Brad Lohaus with to the Kings for center Joe Kleine and forward Ed Pinckney. Right idea, wrong combination, as the newcomers did not solve any of the team's long-term needs up front, while Ainge still had a half dozen years left in the NBA, happily knocking down threes all over the place.

Trading Kevin McHale or, before the season began, Bird, might have kept the club in contention for a title, but no one either had the guts to do so or became convinced that the current group had one more title in it. To do so clashed with Red Auerbach's philosophy at any rate: "You don't trade guys like that. Did we ever trade a Russell, or a Cousy, or a Heinsohn, or a Ramsey? No. You don't get back full value for those kinds of players."

Rodgers did perceive the value in young Reggie Lewis, inserting him into the forward spot and receiving 18.5 points per game in return. Rookie Brian Shaw showed promise at guard, earning second-team All-Rookie recognition and placing second in assists per game behind only Dennis Johnson. The club still had Parish, McHale, and D.J.—when they did not have to sit with injuries—and the bench often played well, but this team floundered on the road; on one six-game trip they went 1–5, a recurring pattern.

Meandering to a 42–40 regular season record, Boston placed third in the Atlantic Division and bowed to the Pistons in a three-game sweep in the first round of the Eastern Conference playoffs.

By way of silver linings, by not rushing Larry Bird back after his surgery, their superstar was poised to return healthy for the next campaign, and he did not like what he saw while recuperating: "We had our butts kicked, but now it's time to turn around and for the Celtics to kick some butt."

1989–90

Il Messaggero Roma. It sounded so romantic to the untrained ear, but to Red Auerbach, Celtics GM Jan Volk, and the Celtics front office, it translated into a major international migraine. The Celtics' promising rookie guard, Brian Shaw, had signed a one-year contract with Boston, and after the spring of 1989 technically enjoyed free agent status outside of the NBA. Seeing Duke's Danny Ferry sign a very lucrative contract with the Italian club Il Messaggero Roma, Shaw's agent commenced negotiations with that team, successfully, as it occurred.

The Celtics went ballistic; Auerbach and Volk seriously did not believe it would happen and thought that they had the right to at least try and match the offer. They did not. In the ignorance-is-bliss category, coach Jimmy Rodgers did not know about the defection until after he returned from a fishing trip in Ontario, Canada. Welcome back!

As always, Larry Bird restored perspective to Celtics Nation, distilling the situation thus: "Would you rather lose Brian Shaw or get Larry Bird back?"

Oddly enough, Boston lost on both ends of the Atlantic and the argument with respect to international acquisitions. They had drafted Yugoslavian forward Dino Radja and signed him despite the player's previous agreement with a European team. A local federal judge ruled against Boston. Although the Celtics still largely dominated on the basketball court, in the legal courts they fared less well during this era.

Dennis Johnson's last year with the club coincided with the dawn of monster scoring from Larry Bird (24.3) and Kevin McHale (20.9).

The team sat in decent draft position that year, 13th overall, but squandered the pick on BYU forward Michael Smith, chosen right before Tim Hardaway, a bitter pill for Jimmy Rodgers, who wanted a guard. Perhaps the front office determined the team had enough point guards and wanted a forward to spell Bird and McHale; Shawn Kemp, Vlade Divac, and Clifford Robinson were all still on the board. Burned by Len Bias, the team gravitated to the one choice whose only vice was an inability to play at the NBA level.

With Bird, the team won 10 more games than it had the previous year, and in the first round of the Eastern Conference playoffs, Boston drew the Knicks, the Pat Ewing–led club that it had lost to only once in their regular matchups. The series started very well for Boston, winning its first two games, scoring 157 points in the second.

Then the Knicks won the next three games and eliminated the Celtics—humiliated them, really. For several years, the Celtics ranked last in the NBA (with one exception, which was a second-to-last effort) in forcing turnovers, and this team needed to create them to compete. The Knicks had not defeated the Celtics at the Boston Garden since 1984 (a skein of 26 straight contests), but in the final game of the series they reversed that trend. Boston turned the ball over constantly. Out with the old.

Jimmy Rodgers continued to chide his team, even Bird. Larry, who fished with Rodgers back in French Lick, "felt bad, because sometimes Jimmy wore his emotions on his sleeve, and that affected the team." On May 8, the Celtics fired Jimmy Rodgers after only two years as their coach.

chapter 28

Long Day's Journey into Night

1990–91

Everyone seemed to support the hiring of Dave Gavitt as the new chief operations officer of the Celtics. A Providence College legend both as a coach and athletics director, he helped form the Big East Conference and stood poised to succeed in the professional arena. Of course, the club already had a general manager in Jan Volk and a de facto general manager in Red Auerbach, but Red fended off any concerns, maintaining, "I will still have the last word, but there will be no problem. There will be no disputes. I recommended Dave. When we met last week to talk about the job, Dave felt the same way. We're old friends. We think alike. We believe in the same things—things the Celtics have stood for over the years. We think alike on how the game should be played, the type of guys you want on your team."

The process of hiring Gavitt delayed the search for a new coach to replace Jimmy Rodgers, but once anointed, Gavitt went right to work to sign up Duke coach Mike Krzyzewski. It came close, but Coach K demurred after considerable wining and dining, leaving Gavitt to hire his clear second choice, Chris Ford. Ford had survived in a twilight zone as an assistant coach without portfolio after Rodgers' termination, waiting for an assignment. Despite never having served as a head coach anywhere, he had played with the Celtics, had waited his turn as an assistant, and had earned the trust of his superiors and the players. He was a good choice.

Philosophically, Auerbach and Gavitt avoided massive changes in the roster, signing up 7'2" Yugoslavian center Stojko Vrankovic and former UNC forward Dave Popson. Like Winston Churchill with the British Empire, Gavitt assured Celtics Nation, "I'm not here to bankrupt the present team." Some rumormongers had Robert Parish going to Seattle, but that never happened, and with its only draft pick, the team chose Dee Brown, a guard out of Jacksonville. Brown was named first-team All-Rookie but Vrankovic and Popson largely failed at spelling Parish, Larry Bird, and Kevin McHale. This development encouraged the further development of Reggie Lewis and Kevin Gamble, and those players blossomed into the team's best scorers. After so much bad news, Brian Shaw returned from his one year with Il Messaggero.

In March, Charles Smith hit two young Boston University students with his car on Commonwealth Avenue. A year later he was sentenced to four and a half years in prison, having been convicted of four misdemeanor charges for hit-and-run driving in the deaths of the female students. In 2010, Smith survived after a lone gunman shot him twice in the chest.

The veterans responded better to Ford's leadership, winning the Atlantic Division with a 56–26 record, which deceives because Bird missed a month in early 1991 due to back issues with the team then at 26–5. Initially reported as spasms, Gavitt went into considerable detail concerning Bird's diagnosis, which made anyone with a shred of empathy cringe. All told, Bird missed more than a quarter of the season but starred when he returned against the Indiana Pacers in the first round of the playoffs.

The fifth game was classic Bird. The series was knotted with the deciding game at the Garden. Diving after a ball with 4:23 left in the second quarter, Bird landed on his right cheekbone and did not move. Worrywarts, also known as everyone in Celtics Nation, froze, believing their hero's back had disabled him again. In his absence, Robert Parish and Reggie Lewis furiously kept their team in the game until, with less than seven minutes left in the third, Bird came running out onto the floor. After a couple tentative minutes he knocked down everything, leading the Celtics to a three-point win and a ticket to the Eastern Conference semis against the defending NBA champion Detroit Pistons.

That year Larry Bird joined only four other players in NBA history with more than 20,000 points and 5,000 assists.

Detroit did not have a great team that year and had begun a gradual decline, which in three years culminated in a 20–62 record, but in this series they had just enough to win in six against a wounded Celtics club. McHale was playing in pain, Bird's back ached, and Robert Parish sat out the sixth game with a sprained ankle. If Larry, Kevin, and Robert were coming through any door, it was probably at the Massachusetts General ER.

Still, with their team finishing first in the Atlantic Division with the fourth-finest record in the NBA, Celtics fans harbored hope that like the 1960s teams, this edition might transition itself into future greatness with promising young players such as Reggie Lewis and rookie point guard Dee Brown. Plus, the big three of Bird, Parish, and McHale still roamed the frontcourt.

1991–92

A likeable team in many ways, the 1991–92 Celtics never threatened to have championship pretension, due to injuries to Bird and McHale, but Reggie Lewis became an All-Star, playing more than 3,000 minutes and scoring more than 1,700 points. Parish continued to play well for a man approaching his 40th birthday. Long-forgotten Celtic Kevin Gamble also stepped up his game.

Boston pushed the Cavaliers to seven games in the Eastern semis, but that was it. The NBA of Larry Bird and Magic Johnson had passed, now in the sole possession of Michael Jordan and the Bulls.

One Celtic did play well in the postseason, as Larry Bird participated in the Olympics as part of the first Dream Team. He almost did not make it, injuries preventing him from playing in some of the prelims leading up to Barcelona. The team won gold, of course, but Bird had played his last game, retiring in mid-August, sacrificing millions of dollars in the process.

Now the Celtics would be Reggie Lewis' team.

1992–93

If you were fortunate enough to watch Kevin McHale in his prime, his final season saddened many, because he played in agony the entire time and worse, had to play tentatively to suit up at all. As Robert Parish quipped, "Kevin is trying to make $10 million moves on $10 ankles."

Marcus Webb had not played his senior year at Alabama—anyone who knew why never told. No one drafted him, but the Celtics signed him as a free agent in 1992, not because they were desperate or anything. Webb missed a team practice, supposedly because the police had pulled him over, but no department had any record of this occurring. The team dropped him on March 17, 1993, on the eve of his arrest for two assaults of women. In July he pled guilty to an assault on his former girlfriend and received a 30-day sentence. In his nine games in the NBA, he scored 39 points. The club fared no better with its first-round draft choice, Jon Barry, who never played in Boston as he sat out in a contract dispute, a stalemate relieved only when the Bucks traded for him (the Celtics acquiring Alaa Abdelnaby in the process).

Reggie Lewis continued to assume his responsibilities as the team's leader, pacing the club in points scored while shooting in the top 10 league-wide in free throw percentage. Promising point guard Sherman Douglas left the team briefly in December, taking off his shoes and socks as the club won an overtime game against the Timberwolves. Douglas took a leave of absence but later returned to the team and became a good playmaker.

Underestimated as a high school and college basketball player, Reggie Lewis became a star with the Celtics. Had he and Len Bias played together, the club could have been a force well into the 1990s.

Seemingly, Chris Ford had successfully dealt with personnel issues as his charges closed out at 48–34, second in the Atlantic Division. And then in the first game of the playoffs, against the Charlotte Hornets, it all fell apart. In the first quarter, Reggie Lewis collapsed as he ran down the left side of the parquet, staggering like a giant invisible hand started pressing him to the floor. Pain aficionados undoubtedly can find tape of it somewhere, but if you watched it live or on television at the time and saw the way he fell, it was unsettling. Lewis came back twice briefly and did score 17 points in 13 minutes to lead his team to a victory, but he knew what it was, admitting, "I started having flashbacks to that Hank Gathers thing." Gathers had died on the court while playing for Loyola Marymount, diagnosed with a fatal heart attack spurred by a cardiac arrhythmia. Cardiac arrhythmia. By summer's end, all Boston fans sadly learned what that medical term meant.

The night the Celtics drafted Reggie Lewis, someone tried to hand him a Celtics hat. Reflexively, Lewis refused to touch it, remembering how Len Bias appeared on his draft night, donning a bright green hat hours before his death, not wanting to invite a comparison.

After the loss, Lewis was taken for a battery of tests at the New England Baptist Hospital, supervised by a Dream Team of cardiologists who concluded that Lewis had a very sick heart, and he sat out the remainder of the playoffs.

Once more unto the breach came the indomitable Kevin McHale. Having endured another pain-filled season, punctuated by back spasms for the final three weeks, he played some of the bravest basketball in his career. In the second game against Charlotte, a narrow Boston defeat, he scored 30 points, pulled down 10 rebounds, and blocked a shot. In the third game, playing just half the time, he scored 15 with five rebounds. In the final game, his team's third and final loss, he blocked three shots and scored 19. McHale retired as one of the greatest players in the history of the NBA.

Bill Walton once called Kevin McHale the best low-post scorer this side of Kareem Abdul-Jabbar. Few would disagree.

Back in Boston, it already had become more than strange. Lewis discharged himself from his hospital care and turned himself over to the care of Brigham and Women Hospital, whereupon Dr. Gilbert Mudge soon proclaimed that Reggie Lewis "had a normal athlete's heart." Subsequent malpractice litigation demonstrated that the more Mudge saw of his patient, the greater his concern became.

Lewis' condition was indeed grave, and while he was casually shooting baskets at Brandeis University, he went into cardiac arrest and died, almost three months after his last game as a Celtic.

After Reggie Lewis was admitted to the hospital, Red Auerbach was admitted into another Boston hospital for his own heart problems. Lewis' fall against Charlotte did not occur in isolation; back in March he had experienced a dizzy spell that had not seemed too serious at the time. Auerbach recovered and played a pivotal role in orchestrating the Reggie Lewis memorial.

1993–94

Robert Parish, the final link to the 1986 team, played better than most of his younger teammates as the team staggered to a 32–50 record this season.

On March 4, Dino Radja scored 36 and pulled down 15 boards against the Lakers, thereby snapping a 13-game Celtics losing streak. "Such is the stuff," as David Bowie once sang, "from where dreams are woven."

Remember the Celtics' farewell dinners at the Hotel Lenox under Red Auerbach? At the Celtics' breakup fete this year, Robert Parish, Sherman Douglas, Alaa Abdelnaby, Kevin Gamble, Ed Pinckney, and Xavier McDaniel did not even show up. An unnamed Celtics official commented, "You can now see how much Larry [Bird] held everything together. On and off the court."

Soon after, David Gavitt had his powers restricted, and then he lost them altogether as M.L. Carr took over basketball operations. By dint of their crummy record, the Celtics drafted ninth after the bloodbath ended, selecting promising center Eric Montross from the University of North Carolina.

1994–95

Dominique Wilkins had bedeviled the Celtics for years, principally with his battles against Bird, so the club signed him as a free agent, using the departing Robert Parish's cap money. Parish learned about his tenure's end from a message left on his phone by M.L. Carr.

Events foreshadowed the doom of this signing. That summer Wilkins had participated in the Olympics as part of the second Dream Team, but coach Don Nelson kept him off the floor to an embarrassing extent. Also, although he had enjoyed another monster season scoring the previous year (26.0 points per game), the Hawks had traded him *and a draft choice* for Danny Manning. Plus, he was in his midthirties.

It looked like a good signing, though, and with the addition of all-time tease Pervis Ellison to the frontcourt of Eric Montross, Dino Radja, and Xavier McDaniel, the Celtics seemed to have solved most of their problems in that area.

But the team never gelled, and finally, after a dispiriting exhibition against the Hawks in January, Chris Ford publicly popped off: "It's tough when you have to play shorthanded. I want to play guys who are working. The second unit went out there and got the job done. They were energized. It's a shame that these guys [the starters] let their egos get in the way. They let their big egos get in the way, and I end up playing shorthanded."

Wilkins shot back, but he muted the effect by his poor defense and continued declining level of play.

Never forget how great Dominique Wilkins was—he remains one of the relatively few NBA players to average 25 points per game for 10 consecutive seasons.

Bizarrely, the Celtics made the playoffs despite their 35–47 record, though Shaquille O'Neal and Penny Hardaway of the Magic disposed of them quickly. On May 5, the Celtics lost at home, ending their playoff series against Orlando and retiring the Boston Garden to professional basketball history. Finally, a new structure would emerge behind it, replete with unobstructed seating, air conditioning, luxury boxes, and wonderful laser shows. An anachronism in its own time, the old Garden would not be salvaged or repackaged like Fenway Park across town; too many shortcomings damned it.

In a mutual dance of death with the woeful Celtics franchise, Wilkins staged a desertion of his three-year contract to join a Greek team, Panathinaikos. Even with hindsight, the Celtics still should have made this deal. They gave nothing up and signed a player coming off an All-Star season in a cap-friendly manner. Even though he did not provide what he promised, Wilkins still led the team in scoring, and due to his machinations, he did not burn the Celtics for the last two years of his contract. It was a one-and-done mistake.

Ironically, the Celtics' success at drawing fans sounded their arena's death knell. During the Bill Russell years, if you bought obstructed seats, you could move up to good vacant seats. Air conditioning and luxury boxes? No one had them until everyone else had them. The Garden housed memories, but now the site is a charmless parking area, with not even a couple of basketball nets set up. Symbolically it marked the end of an unprecedented era of team success in Boston, as clubs in Foxboro and Fenway geared up for titles of their own.

At the conclusion of the season, M.L. Carr supposedly conducted a worldwide search for a new coach, only to choose himself in the end, a long and overwrought process that offended many former Celtics who vied for the position.

1995–96

M.L. Carr attempted to inject his considerable enthusiasm into a franchise that did not excite any in others. In this dreadful era, Boston did pull off one of its greatest trades, sending Eric Montross and a draft pick to the Dallas Mavericks in June for their top picks in the next two drafts. Carr used the first pick on Antoine Walker, a huge upgrade, and the next year the club obtained Ron Mercer.

Other than that, this is the year that Todd Mundt became the first Celtic to ever wear No. 51 on his jersey. That is how boring this team was.

chapter 29

Fellowship of the Miserable

1996–97

Statistically the worst team in franchise history, it is widely conceded that the 1996–97 Boston Celtics laid down for a lottery pick, hoping for the chance to draft Tim Duncan and return the team to a skein of championships.

In the meantime, the team bounced from one losing streak to another, despite a promising first season with Antoine Walker and steals made all over the court by Rick Fox, one of the last links to the previous era. Walker led the team in points scored and rebounds, David Wesley played well at point, and Providence College's Eric Williams possessed a nicer scoring touch than most people expected, but this team was constructed to fail.

What a mess; the roster was otherwise populated by players that should have been superstars but never were (Alton Lister and Pervis Ellison) or seemed like they were okay at a statistical glance but were horrible (Todd Day, Dino Radja, and Dee Brown). Players fought with one another, and assistant coach Dennis Johnson almost quit in the middle of a game. One expected M.L. Carr to pry Curtis Rowe or Sidney Wicks out of retirement or engineer a deal with the Mavericks for a Fred Roberts farewell tour.

Injuries ravaged an already weak team, so severely in fact that in a practice in November, they had to enlist assistant coach John Kuester, donning a turtleneck beneath his jersey, as the 10th player. Frank

Brickowski, signed to replace Eric Montross, injured his shoulder and played only 17 games.

There is little about the season itself worth mentioning. Those of us unfortunate to have had tickets for home games went to see the stars from other teams play.

The team indeed ended up in the lottery and then hired its savior, Kentucky coach Rick Pitino, in May 1997. Out went Red Auerbach as president. Larry Bird, out. Jan Volk, out. Scouts Rick Weitzman and Jon Jennings, out. M.L. Carr, reassigned.

Everyone—*everyone*—felt Rick Pitino was destined to become the next Red Auerbach, with the possible exception of Red Auerbach himself. In retrospect, it seems as if the team owners, the Gastons, had perpetrated an elaborate hoax on Celtics Nation—after all, had not Pitino underwhelmed in his previous incarnation as a head coach with the Knickerbockers, posting an indifferent 90–74 record? And since when does a professional basketball coach have that much influence over the outcome of his team's season, or perhaps more aptly put, how many wins does even a great coach account for each year?

It mattered little. Pitino had the Midas touch, so the legend went. He first came to Boston to coach at Boston University, and as soon as he became its head coach, he returned that program to the NCAA tournament for the first time in almost a quarter-century. Then he jumped to Providence, where he inherited an 11–20 team and restored it to the NCAA tournament as well. Forget the Knicks for a moment; he also took over the Kentucky Wildcats program after Eddie Sutton had butchered it and brought them a national championship and to the NCAA finals in the spring of 1997.

He loved everything about Boston—the bricks, the dirty water, and most of all the championship banners. He wrote a book called *Success Is a Choice*, because he was a winner and he had chosen success.

All the old local Celtics returned for the coronation, and Pitino, a keen student of Celtics history, struck all the right chords, fitting for the Hub's biggest rock star since Aerosmith's Steven Tyler. Dammit, Bob

Cousy, you are going to see another banner in those rafters, he promised, and all who came believed. The Celtics should have staged his introduction to Boston on the Bank of the River Charles, so he could have walked on the water to Cambridge.

Then on May 19, reality began to set in as the Celtics did not win the first or even second pick in the draft: their two first-round choices would occur at Nos. 3 and 6. As much as it hurts to say so, given his later comments about Celtics Nation, had Rick Pitino started with the first draft pick and brought in Tim Duncan, he might have brought one or more titles to Boston, no matter whom he picked with the second lottery pick that year. The cynic might suggest that the same might hold true for M.L. Carr, but no, Pitino was not so much a bad coach as he was a poor GM. The Gastons had given him almost full power over the franchise, and he simply did not know how to assemble a championship club without Tim Duncan falling into his lap.

On the same date that his Louisville Cardinals won the NCAA championship in 2013, it was announced that Rick Pitino had been elected to the Basketball Hall of Fame, thereby joining former Celtics coaches Honey Russell and Doggie Julian as men selected for their excellence as college basketball coaches.

Plus, the Celtics were in Cap Hell, with approximately 80 percent of their salary space dedicated to seven players, none of them stars.

Not able to choose Duncan on draft night—or even Keith Van Horn, taken with the second pick—Pitino settled for Colorado point guard Chauncey Billups and his protégé at Kentucky, Ron Mercer. Billups was a great choice, a player who had a better career than Van Horn. Mercer was the best choice out there, unless one had foreseen the potential of Tracy McGrady out of high school. Not a bad draft, but the Celtics still lacked a center, unless one counted Pervis Ellison, and no one did.

That is when Pitino the coach first catered to his dark side, the director of operations who could not direct operations well. He correctly began by renouncing the contracts of numerous players, with Rick Fox the lone bit of talent sacrificed, but then made a huge blunder by signing Travis Knight ("He's going to be a great, great player in this league," Pitino assured) as the center of the future. Knight had demonstrated little during his rookie season in L.A., but Pitino panicked over perceived need and lost his bet heavily.

Pitino did get rid of Dino Radja, a good move, a skin rash that never seemed to go away, but the next three signings—Andrew DeClerq, Bruce Bowen, and Tony Massenburg—thrilled no one. Even worse, Pitino traded promising Eric Williams for two second-round draft choices and then squandered those choices too.

The savior had essentially re-created the Celtics roster from two years previous.

1997–98

In defense of Antoine Walker, the man played some of the most minutes in Celtics history this side of Bill Russell, scored a lot of points (1,840 in his second season in the league), rebounded well on both ends of the court, and stole the ball quite a bit. Rick Pitino claimed that unless the Bulls offered him Michael Jordan, Walker was untradeable.

Other aspects of Walker's game irritated Celtics fans as time wore on. He shot and missed too many threes, philanthropically turned the ball over to his opponents, and wiggled when he made shots. Like Drew Bledsoe of the Patriots, every year he seemed to backslide just a little bit until he drove everyone nuts, but he starred for his former Wildcats coach in their reunion year and did participate in three All-Star Games in his first seven professional seasons. In an era when most Celtics fans did not know the difference between Zan Tabak and Vic Tayback, Walker alone distinguished himself.

As part of the Celtics' new no-nonsense style, Rick Pitino took his charges down to an old military base in Newport, Rhode Island, to train.

If ever a man came to Boston in the wrong era, it was Antoine Walker. Had he played under Red Auerbach with no three-point temptation, Antoine may have made the Hall of Fame—or at least received a kick in the pants from Red every time the player wiggled after making a basket.

Pitino did reunite with another Kentucky player, Walter McCarty, in a deal with the Knicks, adding a useful backup at forward and perhaps the all-time leader in Tommy Points (punctuated with broadcaster Tommy Heinsohn exclaiming, "I love Waltah!"). The season started off promisingly enough as Walker scored 31 points as the Celtics defeated Michael Jordan's Bulls, but then Boston lost its next five games and the buzzards started circling Rick Pitino.

Of course, Pitino saw to that, trading Chauncey Billups in February in a multiplayer deal with Toronto, obtaining Kenny Anderson as the principal player in return. Old wounds nagged Anderson, then in his seventh NBA season, and he ended up playing more than half the games in a season only twice in his five years in Boston. Billups, of course, proceeded to make five All-Star teams and win a Finals MVP Award as a member of the Pistons. Unfortunately, it was not the worst trade Pitino ever executed.

The Celtics staggered to a 36–46 finish, considered by some to constitute an achievement, considering how relatively little talent the coach had to work with. One piece of luck did fall to Rick Pitino during his early reign: on June 24, he drafted Paul Pierce.

1998–99

A lockout threatened to wipe out the entire 1998–99 season, but unfortunately for Rick Pitino and the Celtics, NBA labor and management came together and staged a 50-game season that commenced in February 1999. The team stopped practicing at Brandeis in favor of their secluded, state-of-the-art facility in Waltham, complete with a parquet floor and top training, medical, and rehabilitation facilities in house.

During the lockout, Pitino suckered L.A. into taking Travis Knight for Tony Battie. Simply put, Knight was not even an adequate backup NBA center, while Battie played very well for Boston for more than five years. On the other side of the ledger, as soon as the truncated season started, Pitino made a stinker trade, swapping Andrew DeClerq and a future first-round draft choice to Cleveland for center Vitaly Potapenko. Potapenko proved a disappointment to the team while Cleveland used the pick for guard Andre Miller, who as of 2013 was approaching 16,000 points scored in his career.

Rookie Paul Pierce led the team in points while Antoine Walker set the pace for rebounds, signifying the utter absence of a credible physical presence at center. The team won 19 games and Pitino started reacting, telling one heckler to shut up and lose his gut. Having welcomed Kenny Anderson to the club, he now feuded with his veteran point guard, keeping him from flying to a game due to perceived insubordination.

As bad as it got for Anderson, Pitino singled out Pierce for much of his wrath, not so much coaching him as indiscriminately dumping on him. Even when the coach spread the blame, he did not view his own shortcomings: "Our team is not doing well at all. We can't guard the low post. We don't guard screens well. We have five different players who can't guard anyone. You should see the way we're grading out for these games. I have never had a team grade out so low."

These comments occurred in the midst of a 1–10 stretch. Cedric Maxwell, now a Celtics radio analyst, said it much more succinctly: "I think I'm going to throw up."

Antoine Walker, to his credit, held down his lunch and some of his friends' meals too, reportedly arriving at training camp 38 pounds overweight. Boston boo birds showered him with abuse, and Walker responded to the pressure with some truly horrible nights from the floor—for example, 1-for-14 against Kevin Garnett and the Timberwolves, 2-for-15 versus the Bulls—and so it went.

Pitino had passed from his honeymoon period into a hopeless marriage in less than two years, as some fans demanded the return of the good old days under M.L. Carr.

After this awful season ended, the Celtics paid tribute to Bill Russell by re-retiring his number in a public display of affection for a man who contributed so much to a once proud franchise. For Boston, the past was glorious.

1999–2000

On March 1, 2000, after a galling loss to the Toronto Raptors, Rick Pitino went off on one of the most famous rants since Sam Adams roamed the Boston Waterfront:

> We've played hard the whole year, and we are being positive every day. You're the ones who are being negative. Larry Bird is not walking through that door, fans. Kevin McHale is not walking through that door, and Robert Parish is not walking through that door. And if you expect them to walk through that door, they are going to be gray and old.

He blasted the fans and media for their negativity, producing a loser's lament as timeless in its own inverse fashion as Knute Rockne's "Win one for the Gipper" speech.

Rick Pitino was turning weird.

Witness another poor trade he made in the summer, dumping Ron Mercer and others for Danny Fortson and a couple of spare parts. From afar, Chauncey Billups had this to say about Mercer and his former coach: "I thought Ron would be there for the majority of his career. But as I thought more and more, Pitino is a cold individual, man. There really is not that much loyalty in that Boston organization, I don't feel like. I know there's a lot of other guys that feel the same way I do."

Blown out by Orlando in late March, in the midst of a 10-game losing streak, Pitino threatened to suspend players but never did.

Antoine Walker did not quit, though he did articulate his teammates' frustration by conceding, "It's very hard, and it's very difficult. But right now we can't afford to feel sorry for ourselves, because this is not the way we want to end the season. This is not the positive way to end our season. This is not the way we want our fans to see us at the end of the season."

Antoine kept trying, scoring 20.5 points per game and leading Boston in rebounds as Pierce added 19.5 points per game. On some nights, with a little help from their teammates, they seemed like the foundation for the next Celtics resurrection. It was coming, not fast enough perhaps for Pitino, but for at least one of the club's young stars, a championship season was on the horizon.

2000–01

It looked very bleak for Paul Pierce on September 25, 2000, at the Buzz Club near the Theatre District, after assailants stabbed him 11 times in the face, chest, and back, supposedly as he tried to break up a fight. Fortunately, the stabbings did not sever an artery, and after lung surgery, Pierce recovered and played every game in the ensuing season.

Rick Pitino gave us numerous memorable quotes during his tenure at the Garden, but one long-forgotten nugget may have been his finest. Undiplomatically, Pitino described the play of rookie Jerome Moiso thusly: "He's not ready from an intensity level. He's not ready from a defensive level. Basically, he's not ready for pro basketball." That's what happens when one succumbs to the fellowship of the miserable.

Ironically, if Rick Pitino had stood by his players and held onto someone like Chauncey Billups, he would have had enough expiring contracts to pursue a top free agent or at the least begun to benefit from the team's maturation. Instead, he now had too many average players around to augment Pierce and Walker, and he had one fewer good man at his disposal in early November when Kenny Anderson sustained a broken jaw against Cleveland. Gamely, Anderson stayed in the game, but once the severity of his injury was diagnosed, he had his jaw wired shut.

The Rick Pitino death watch extended through the holiday and then mercifully ended after the team staggered to a 12–22 start. The coach stayed behind in Florida to consider his options; then on January 8, 2001, he pulled down the curtain on his failed experience in Boston. After another dispiriting defeat, a 112–86 mauling from the Heat, his team flew back to Logan Airport without him.

Assistant Jim O'Brien took over and restored stability to the team, winning 24 and losing 24 to bring another dispiriting season to an end. Without Pitino, the Boston Celtics in the very next year would not only make the playoffs but advance to the Eastern Conference Finals. Who needs saviors anyway?

chapter 30
Not This Again

2001–02

Briefly, new coach Jim O'Brien contemplated placing Antoine Walker at point guard but reportedly reconsidered, due to intervening rule changes. Too bad; perhaps if he'd had Walker at the point, Antoine would not have shot so many damn threes. Regardless of what position he played, the forward no longer had to toil for Rick Pitino, and this freedom, along with the continued maturity of Paul Pierce, spurred Walker onto perhaps his finest professional campaign, leading the team in rebounds and assists.

Only Pierce outscored him—and everyone else in the NBA for that matter—tallying 2,144 points. The Truth seemed to do everything better—shooting fouls, rebounding, playmaking, stealing the ball, and shooting threes with greater confidence—and earned his first All-Star recognition.

Figuring that Kenny Anderson had only so many dribbles left in his tank, the club drafted Joe Johnson from Arkansas and Kedrick Brown from a community college with the 10th and 11th picks in the draft, and took Joseph Forte with the 21st pick.. So many other franchises had prospered by selecting prospects straight out of high school or junior colleges that the Celtics decided to gamble. Johnson became a perennial All-Star elsewhere, while Brown and Forte never successfully bridged the gap.

In retrospect, Antoine Walker, like Rasheed Wallace later, proved that shooting threes should not be an impulse, but this year the Celtics largely lived by them, with Pierce and Walker firing up more than 1,100 of them combined. So did their supporting cast, which included Erick Strickland, Walter McCarty, and returning Celtic Eric Williams. The fast-breaking Celtics of yore became the three-heaving team in transition, and it worked well enough to place them second overall in the Atlantic Division with a 49–33 record.

We have referred to Rick Pitino as the general manager and coach during his tenure in Boston, and it has become fashionable to say Pitino was a great coach but a lousy GM. At least on paper, Chris Wallace served as GM much of the time and survived in that role after Pitino departed. To obtain the services of Wallace, Pitino swapped a second-round pick with Orlando for a lower-ranked second-round pick and the right to sign Wallace.

With the playoffs a distinct possibility for the first time in seven years, the club forged a blockbuster deal in which it traded Joe Johnson, Milt Palacio, Randy Brown, and a future first-rounder for forward Rodney Rogers and guard Tony Delk. In the long term the deal killed the Celtics, but most fans and pundits loved it at the time, with Kenny Anderson sounding one of the few cautionary words: "If I was the general manager, I might have done the same move, but I would have been bothered giving up on Joe Johnson." Largely Celtics Nation celebrated, as Boston now had Pierce, Walker, Rogers, and Eric Williams at forward, together with an experienced and exciting shooting guard to augment Anderson. Along with Tony Battie at center, Boston was competitive again.

The big trade did not immediately improve the team in February, as the Celtics proceeded to lose four straight, but from there until the end of the regular season, they finished strong at 18–6. Rogers helped quite a bit; Delk could not hit the broad side of a barn, never mind the net nailed to it. Tellingly, the Celtics were the worst shooting team in the NBA.

The shooting percentages did not catch up to the young Celtics in the first round of the playoffs against Allen Iverson and the Sixers or when they blew past the Pistons in five to advance to the Eastern Conference Finals.

The Nets of Jason Kidd, Keith Van Horn, Kerry Kittles, and Kenyon Martin, a team that the Celtics nearly swept in the regular season, were waiting for them. This is one of the statistically bewildering series in Celtics history. Even when they won, as they did in Jersey on May 21 to even the series 1–1, Walker shot 11-for-32 and Pierce went 3-for-20, a worse performance than people on freeways at carnivals trying to fire a basketball into a small oval net.

Errant gunning almost caught up with Boston in the next contest, as the Celtics sat 21 points behind the Nets in the fourth quarter. Jim O'Brien huddled his charges, and then Antoine Walker took over, exhorting his teammates to play harder and to attack the Nets in a different way. Then Boston staged one of its greatest comebacks, with Pierce driving through Nets, Rogers hitting on six straight foul shots, Walker challenging everyone and drawing fouls, and Delk hitting a key three. Boston outscored New Jersey 41–16 in the fourth quarter for this most improbable win. Paul Pierce called it back in the locker room: "I don't know what I'd do without Antoine Walker as my teammate. He's one of our emotional leaders. I just saw it in his eyes. He took control of this whole game." Even Red Auerbach thought it was one of the greatest comebacks.

Unfortunately, that marked the high-water mark for this Celtics team, as Jason Kidd and the Nets' defense finally took advantage of Boston's poor shooting, shutting down the Celtics for the privilege of being swept by the Lakers in the NBA Finals. Still, there was every reason to think that next year, Boston would play for the championship.

2002–03

Flush from their successful season, the Celtics front office experienced a collective hangover when they recognized that they would not re-sign Rodney Rogers. Coach Jim O'Brien emphasized Rogers' importance to his team, insisting, "There was a reason that we went 18–6 down the stretch and then went to the finals of the East." Looming luxury tax considerations supposedly kept Boston from re-signing the forward, despite O'Brien's efforts and the pleas of his teammates. By failing to do so, the Celtics repeated their error from years ago when they failed to come to terms with Paul Silas, losing a player whose stats did not adequately convey his immense value to the team.

Faced with the same limitations that had bedeviled them for 10 years, GM Chris Wallace forged a deal with Seattle: Kenny Anderson, Vitaly Potapenko, and seldom-used guard Joseph Forte for Vin Baker and Shammond Williams. Vincent Baker, a minister's son from Old Saybrook, Connecticut, had starred in his first five seasons, an All-Rookie selection and then four straight All-Star Games, plus an appearance in the Olympics. A 6'11" combination of forward and center, he once led the league in minutes played, yet in the previous two seasons his playing time and productivity both had dropped.

As usual, Kenny Anderson sounded the Greek chorus: "They're in trouble for a minute...we'll see how Antoine and Vin work together." Anderson had played commendably, and no one knew at this point that he was washed up, a fate that became apparent after he departed. Potapenko hung around as a reserve for a while, while Forte scored only 24 more points in his career; the Celtics had not given up much, but they ended up getting much less.

Unappreciated at the time, the best deal that summer involved Paul Gaston selling the Celtics to the triumvirate of Irving Grousbeck, Wyc Grousbeck, and Steve Pagliuca, who spearheaded Boston Basketball Partners LLC.

A common thread during these generally poor years in Celtics history is the ownership of the Gastons, a 19-year run of screwups and mishaps. The titular owner Paul Gaston rarely showed his face, and his passing generated few tears. As Paul Pierce explained, "You not only owe it to the team, but you owe it to the fans to communicate, to hear what we have going on and hear what we need.... [Gaston] was one of those guys that was looking from the outside and didn't understand what was going on with the team. Being that we had such a great team and went to the Eastern Conference Finals, he should have listened and done whatever it took to make everybody happy and bring another contending team back. He just seemed like an owner that was never really interested in how many games we won or how many games we lost. He was just more interested in how much money he was making or how much money he lost."

Bringing Baker to Boston ruined the team, as he underperformed with a large contract and many years left on it. As the season regressed, he played sparingly and poorly, not scoring, not rebounding, lost on defense, and picking up fouls like Easter eggs. Finally on February 27, Baker was suspended, felled by his issues with alcohol.

One of the most intense players to ever don a Celtics jersey, Paul Pierce augmented his inside game with an impressive presence on the perimeter as he matured.

The classic requiem on Vin Baker, of course, came from Bill Walton: "I turned 50. I've had 32 operations, had an endless string of stress fractures and two fused ankles. I can still play better than Vin Baker."

The Baker situation obscured the achievements of his teammates, particularly Pierce. The Pacers' Al Harrington observed Paul was "even better this year than last year. His handle is unbelievable. He's using both hands, going behind the back, doing whatever it takes to bring the ball up. I'm impressed. He could always shoot, but the ballhandling is just another dimension he's added. Most great players do that: they add something new every year."

The estimable Tony Battie played well at center despite a bum knee, and Walter McCarty continued as a fan favorite and leading recipient of Tommy Heinsohn's accolades. Delk came up lame a lot with an injured ankle and never scored as consistently as anyone wished. The team that had participated in the Eastern Conference Finals had evaporated.

Baker's demise deflected some of the criticism of former punching bag Antoine Walker, but Toine's game had deteriorated, barraging the basket with field goals and threes which, with increasing frequency, did not ever become field goals or threes. He also lost time to a faulty knee.

In the playoffs the Celtics slipped by the Pacers but got swept by the Nets at home, while newly appointed GM Danny Ainge viewed the wreckage.

2003–04

Vin Baker was the feel-good story of Celtics camp, fit and determined to contribute, an impression punctuated by Jim O'Brien, who told the press, "I expect leadership from him, added low-post scoring, a much more effective defensive player, a much more effective rebounder. In short, I expect him to be like a new player for us, like we just went out and were able to sign a free agent that is the type of Vin Baker that we saw in the past. How quickly he'll be able to acclimate himself remains to be seen. But I think we'll see a strong addition in Vin Baker."

Danny Ainge did not wait for the season to start to make changes, swapping Antoine Walker and Tony Delk to the Mavericks for Raef LaFrentz, Jiri Welsch, Chris Mills, and a first-round draft choice, later used for Delonte West. GM and star had a brief phone call about the trade and then parted as something less than friends, with Ainge later observing, "Antoine had a grasp on our franchise. If Antoine is Michael Jordan, it's okay to have a grasp. If Antoine is Larry Bird, it's okay to have a grasp, or Bill Russell. I think those players had grasps on their franchises. Shaquille O'Neal has a grasp on the Los Angeles Lakers. But I didn't perceive Antoine's grasp on us as a positive thing."

Expounded Ainge, "I think Antoine Walker is an excellent player and he's done an excellent job in this organization. This is simply basketball. This has nothing to do with anything personal. I don't know Antoine except from basketball observation, from a fan, coaching, and general managing perspective. Maybe I didn't have as high a regard for his game as he had for his game, but I certainly respect Antoine Walker as a player."

In late January, Jim O'Brien resigned as Celtics coach, citing philosophical differences with Ainge. O'Brien stressed defense, Ainge wanted more offense, and the deal that sealed O'Brien's fate occurred before Christmas when Boston traded Eric Williams, Tony Battie, and Kedrick Brown to the Cavaliers for Ricky Davis, Chris Mihm, Yogi Stewart, and a draft choice.

There were other reasons, as Ainge made clear: "Another key to the vision is a greater emphasis on developing young players. I feel like players like Joe Johnson and Chauncey Billups should be able to develop. One of my biggest concerns, as much as I like Walter McCarty and Mark Blount, was letting them play 40 minutes against Kenyon Martin while Chris Mihm, Brandon Hunter, and Kendrick Perkins sat. It's not only shortsighted, it's obstinate. And not playing Marcus Banks more than 10 minutes is unproductive to our vision."

Under interim coach John Carroll, the Celtics lost 12 of their next 13 games, though they did play well in spurts later on. Despite finishing the regular season at 36–46, the Celtics participated in the playoffs where the Pacers of Jermaine O'Neal and Reggie Miller swept them. Besides Paul

Pierce, the Celtics started Mark Blount, Chucky Atkins, Jiri Welsch, and Walter McCarty, making it perhaps the least distinguished playoff group since Honey Russell roamed courtside chiding his players to contain the Chicago Stags.

This team was all Paul Pierce, as he outscored his nearest teammate by almost 1,000 points as Boston was swept in the first round of the playoffs. It seemed like another long day's journey into night for the hapless Celtics.

chapter 31
Youth Movement

2004–05

It all makes perfect sense now—combining a basketball operations head who had a coach quit on him with a former coach who did not get along with his last general manager. They first became friends playing together in the 1988 All-Star Game, and wisely, Danny Ainge hired Doc Rivers as the new Celtics head coach, succeeding interim coach John Carroll.

Boston had endured two false messiahs since Larry Bird's back had begun to ache, Dave Gavitt and Rick Pitino, and despite each man's talents and accomplishments outside of Causeway Street, each had failed here miserably. Doc had coached Orlando for four full seasons, fired when his team started out the fifth year at 1–10. He had made the play-offs three of those years before bowing out in the first round each time.

This time, the hiring of a new Celtics coach invited scrutiny, with fans and pundits divided on the merits, though few really loved it or hated it.

Skepticism.

Fortuitously, Ainge and Rivers not only had cultivated mutual respect, but they also shared a vision for turning the team into a championship contender. Initially, they instituted an up-tempo offense, not a bad idea for such a young team, and in the draft it kept getting younger, with three players chosen in the first round: St. Joseph's guard Delonte West, Oklahoma State's shooting guard Tony Allen, and 19-year-old Al Jefferson.

Somewhat incongruously it also got older, signing Tom Gugliotta.

Outside of Paul Pierce, Rivers and Ainge faced a number of riddles on the roster. The Celtics had overpaid Mark Blount at center, but would he at least provide the club with the same body of work he compiled by the spring of 2004? Behind him stood Kendrick Perkins, a year removed from high school, attempting to advance his career along the learning curve. The team also had a former center, Raef LaFrentz, who had played only 17 games the past year before undergoing surgery in his right knee, now hopefully reviving his career. Did newly acquired Gary Payton have anything left at point guard? Would Marcus Banks ever contribute adequately at that position?

But the biggest question mark revolved around guard Ricky Davis, whose prowess as a pain in the ass always seemed to exceed his considerable talents as a scorer.

Through late February, the inability to successfully solve these issues consigned the Celtics to a 27–28 record. In a particularly ugly display, the Nuggets blew them out, as the Celts rang up four separate technical fouls in the final 0.3 in the first half, Doc Rivers earning his first ejection. The next day, the Celtics answered some of those riddles by executing a blockbuster deal with the Hawks to reacquire Antoine Walker (and a player to be named later), in exchange for Gary Payton, Tom Gugliotta, Yogi Stewart, and a first-round draft choice. Mere months ago, Walker had accused Danny Ainge of trading him to the Mavericks out of spite, desiring only to derail his career, but to their credit they both saw that this move would strengthen the Celtics, as Boston basically traded away a draft choice and expiring contracts; Gary Payton was the player to be named later in the Walker deal, whom Atlanta released and Boston promptly re-signed on March 1. Gary Payton was traded for Gary Payton. Better yet, the draft pick that Boston traded away, after some complicated maneuvering down the road, eventually came back to them in the person of Rajon Rondo. In a smaller deal, they traded guard Jiri Welsch to the Cavs for a draft pick.

Upon his return, prodigal wiggler Walker restored the trust by leading the Celtics with 24 points as they defeated the Jazz and won 11 of their next 12 games. Most important, he rebounded, providing some relief for a team let down particularly by Mark Blount. Rejuvenated, Boston finished the regular season as Atlantic Division champions at 45–37.

One of the finest point guards in NBA history, Gary Payton continued his enigmatic ways as a Celtic, causing Danny Ainge to reflect, "There's certain players that earn certain things and there's a trust that has to develop, and Doc needed Gary's trust because he knew he needed Gary to be a leader, and he needed Gary, so he might have played Gary more minutes than Gary might have deserved. I'm not saying that fit can't happen in the right circumstances. I would say it got better when Gary came back. Doc and Gary had a chance to talk and Gary chose to come back." Ainge did concede that without Payton, the team never would have won as many games as it did. At his best, he brought consistency and professionalism to a young club. Once after flying to California to help his sick mother, he returned in a game against the Timberwolves to score 22 points, dishing out seven assists.

Determined to avenge their four-and-out loss to the Pacers in the previous season's playoffs, the Celtics drew Indiana again in what became one of the messiest series in their history. Boston blew out Indy in Game 1 at the Garden, leading by as much as 76–39 at one juncture, then got sloppy; they lost a later contest after Antoine Walker, who had merited a second technical in a mixed martial arts exhibition with Jermaine O'Neal and then pushed aside official Tom Washington to argue with another ref, incurred a one-game suspension. Hub fans bid Antoine adieu.

Down 3–2, Boston looked lost in Indianapolis, particularly after the refs ejected Paul Pierce for waving his arm at Jamaal Tinsley (who flopped like Raggedy Ann), his second technical, a punishment that Pierce responded to by taking his shirt off and waving it defiantly at the Pacers fans. Antoine and Al Jefferson bailed him out, prompting a seventh and deciding game back in the Garden—or whatever corporate complex they called it back then.

Game 7 at the Garden was traditionally an opportunity for every team to create its own legendary moments; instead, the Celtics shot .370 from the floor and got overrun in the third and fourth quarters by a team that they should have defeated with ease.

Clamor erupted to divest the team of Paul Pierce—the guy lacked maturity and composure, it was said. Better to trade him for a star or a bunch of picks. The Celtics ended matters in a maelstrom of embarrassment, necessitating significant changes in the off-season.

2005–06

Fortunately, Danny Ainge and Doc Rivers did not trade Paul Pierce away, but they did let Gary Payton walk, and when it became evident they did not intend on signing Antoine Walker long term, they gravitated into a five-team deal in which they dealt him to Miami and got nothing back of any value.

In lieu of re-signing their veterans, Boston continued to build through the draft, choosing Gerald Green, Ryan Gomes, and Orien Greene. They also signed up free agent Brian Scalabrine, a popular player who now works road games as a Celtics broadcaster.

Pierce thrived, scoring a career-high 26.8 points per game; sad to say it reflected not simply his excellence but the absolute dependence of his teammates on him in the lineup.

They never won more than two games in a row and had to wait until December 21 to accomplish that feat, as they drifted to a 33–49 record.

Blunders like Blount kept the Celtics from seriously contending, as the underperforming center continued to avoid rebounding, an odd aversion for a pivot man to develop. Walker had helped alleviate that deficiency, but now the team had to rely increasingly on Kendrick Perkins.

This team's chronic dreadfulness spurred Ainge on January 26, 2006, to trade Blount, Marcus Banks, Ricky Davis, Justin Reed, and two second-round draft picks to the Timberwolves for Wally Szczerbiak, one-time first pick overall Michael Olowokandi, development leaguer Dwayne Jones, and a first-round draft choice.

This transaction freed up millions of dollars misappropriated to Blount and provided Boston with another shooter in Szczerbiak. By way of a probably unwitting back-door compliment, Danny Ainge explained, "We feel Wally can complement Paul in a different way. Wally is a high-percentage shooter, and he's a better post-up player. But more than anything, he's just different than Ricky." In Szczerbiak, Boston obtained a forward who averaged 17.5 points per game the remainder of the season, picking away from the perimeter.

The move paid immediate dividends as Boston won its next game against the Kings; unfortunately, the team then lost six in a row. It did accelerate the team's transition to a younger roster, as Doc Rivers now had the luxury to play Delonte West, Al Jefferson, Kendrick Perkins, Ryan Gomes, and Tony Allen more often.

It is nearly impossible to unearth anything resembling an amusing anecdote or story concerning this club or its bleak season, but young guard Gerald Green did provoke some smiles on even the most miserable faces in Celtics Nation. After a mandatory afternoon meeting, he flew down to Fayetteville, North Carolina, where he had played in the D League, to haul back some personal valuables before a team practice the next day. He never made it. Missed flights, cancellations, delays (five hours on a commuter plane for a tall young man), and unappreciated needs for connecting flights foiled this ill-conceived plan. Green not only experienced issues in the air, but he also expressed trepidation on water, explaining why he did not want to fish in the rich saltwater off of the New England coast: "Did you see the movie *Titanic?* That was a true story. Icebergs."

Lost in the depressing season was the appreciation of Paul Pierce's growth as a player. Once seen as trade bait, this year he led the club not only in points per game but in rebounds, assists, and steals per game, upping his field goal percentage to a then–personal best of .471. The Celtics did not grow accustomed to victories, but when they prevailed, it often occurred due to a buzzer beater by their best player. Co-owner Wyc Grousbeck appreciated Pierce, pledging, "We don't intend for Paul to go anywhere. Paul has also said that he would like to retire a Celtic, and that is my primary goal. Not only do I want him to retire a Celtic, I want his number retired. I want him to have the kind of career here where he would be the last guy to wear No. 34. The way to have that happen is for us to really do something and for him to keep playing at a high level. That's the goal. Life brings changes. It's not a promise, but it's a hope."

The Celtics stunk, but they still had Paul Pierce, and they extended his contract to keep it that way. Now they needed to get him some teammates of a similar caliber.

2006–07

Red Auerbach died on October 28, 2006. A lot of people knew Red; most did not, even if they thought they did. The fans knew the shtick, but they constituted by far the most populous segment of Celtics Nation, the folks who bought tickets to games or wore out the couch watching the boob tube. Fans hate when the team loses and rejoice when they prevail, and Red Auerbach made them win more often than the guys wearing the other-colored laundry on the court.

A fan knew that Red Auerbach saw the world in Green or in Black; even more so than did Johnny Most, Red wanted the Celtics to win as much as we did. Red did not attend our weddings or graduations, but he showed up at most of the other memorable nights of our lives, lighting up a cigar as the Celtics won another of our championships. If he sometimes acted rudely to people or pissed off opponents with his arrogance, we excused him or, maybe better yet, we thought that we understood him and loved him anyway. After all, that's what happens in good families.

But the Celtics existed before Red coached them or managed their personnel; older fans remember him humiliating the Boston teams of Honey Russell or Doggie Julian. At the other end of the continuum, it's odd to think that Red never saw Kevin Garnett or Ray Allen or Shaquille O'Neal donning the Celtics green or helped to raise another banner. He has been gone that long. But damned if he didn't get the whole tradition started.

Now it was for others, and this 2006–07 team tested our love.

As a reward for their breathtakingly bad play, the Celtics possessed a lottery pick in the draft, so Danny Ainge contacted multiple teams and ended up consummating many deals by draft day. In this vein, they traded the pick along with Raef LaFrentz and Dan Dickau to the Trail Blazers for legendary point guard Sebastian Telfair, Theo Ratliff, and a second-round pick.

This did little for them on the court, as Telfair continued to fail to fulfill his high school hype, and Ratliff, the patron saint of expiring contracts, played only 44 minutes for Boston. It did dump a lot of salary off of Boston's books, and in a poor draft, Boston thankfully did not get burned in losing its lottery selection. Yet if that transaction did little for the Celtics, they scored big by trading a 2007 second-round pick for the Nuggets' second-round pick this year, a talented forward from Cal named Leon Powe.

Not meaning to bury Theo Ratliff but to praise him, how about sending some votes his way for the MVP of the Celtics? Absurd on its face, remember that this player was earning a ridiculous amount of money on an expiring contract, allegedly $11,666,66 yearly. Sure he suited up for Boston only twice and scored only five points and hauled in seven rebounds, but he created some cap maneuverability in the future, enough to help sign a difference-maker. Had he enjoyed a bit of health, he might have been a defensive force for Boston, but from the moment he arrived, his career was hopelessly marred by a bad back.

Then they hit the jackpot, swapping a first-rounder for the ghost of Brian Grant (a money dump, he never played for Boston or anyone else again) and a rookie point guard from Kentucky named Rajon Rondo. They also announced the formation of a dance team.

And they did not stop there, as the front office dreamt of obtaining either Ohio State center Greg Oden or Texas forward Kevin Durant a year hence, in the next draft.

Youth was wasted on the young, as the new-look Celtics staggered, losing six of their first seven games, 5–13 overall, until they went on a five-game winning streak that culminated in a victory over the Bobcats on December 16, when Pierce scored 35. That marked the last time Pierce and Wally Szczerbiak played together for nearly two months, at which time the club totally collapsed.

Szczerbiak had left ankle "structural weakness," and Pierce labored with a stress reaction in his foot and then sustained an elbow infection as Boston's young guns started losing, then *really* losing. In fact, after they defeated the Memphis Grizzlies on January 5, they lost 18 straight, breaking the old franchise mark for futility. At least Gerald Green won the All-Star slam dunk contest in the middle of it all. There was talk about obtaining Allen Iverson, but that went nowhere, as did the Celtics.

John and Connie Simmons, who played for Boston in the 1940s, are mistakenly credited as the only brothers to have played for the Celtics, when in fact they are the only ones to have played *together*. Sebastian Telfair's brother, Jamel Thomas, played briefly for the Green during the 1999–2000 season. Later, their cousin Stephon Marbury suited up for the good guys.

It was a gruesome year to be a Celtics fan as the home team staggered to a 24–58 record, and yet on the streets, sports talk shows, and online chat rooms, the fans had reason to be hopeful. Ten years prior, when the team had last tanked its season to get the first pick in the draft, not everything rose or fell on one player like Tim Duncan. In this draft, both Kevin Durant and Greg Oden were coming out, and it seemed inconceivable that the team would wind up with neither player.

Unlike 1996–97, the club had a superstar in Paul Pierce and one of the best coaches in the NBA in Doc Rivers, not to mention exciting forward Al Jefferson and rookie point guard Rajon Rondo, so some hope for the future existed. Inarguably it was to the team's advantage to maximize its chances on draft day to have the opportunity to obtain the rights to either Oden or Durant. So they reeked, either by design or through dumb luck.

In March 2007, Paul Pierce went to the movies and was immediately recognized by the ticket-taker, not an unexpected occurrence, but the greeting was. The ticket-taker cheerfully stated, "I hope you guys lose," a blasphemous statement if uttered in the 1980s or before but a perfectly acceptable comment for a Celtics fan to make, with the hope that mounting losses would translate into the first pick in the draft. The fan got his wish, as the Celtics squandered an 18-point lead in the fourth quarter against the Bobcats.

Pierce gamely resisted taking the games for granted. Hurt through much of the season, he declined a chance to sit down during a late March double-overtime loss to the Magic, maintaining, "The game was so close that I hate to bail out on my team like that. But [the possibility of leaving the game] was pretty close."

Eventually the team shut down Pierce for the season, but injuries engulfed more than just the star of the team. In an April loss to the Heat, for instance, Boston suited up only eight players. Fittingly enough, the club lost eight of its last nine games. Season over.

Now, for the draft. In a class-laden gesture, Celtics management invited M.L. Carr to attend the live lottery selection program in Secaucus, New Jersey, in May. Carr had scaled the heights in the city as a player and the depths as a coach, but they hoped his luck, and that of the franchise, had changed.

It did not; incredibly, Boston ended up with the fifth selection in the draft. No Durant. No Oden. No new championship banners in the rafters. The superstitious damned the Celtics for allowing cosmically unlucky M.L. Carr anywhere near the live selection, but Boston this time around had a general manager with a plan.

Asked for his reaction to the Celtics not landing one of the top two lottery picks, Danny Ainge replied, "Dang it." A crestfallen Doc Rivers augmented Ainge's comments, deadpanning, "He's Mormon. I said something else."

As we know now, had Boston ended up with one of the top two choices and picked Greg Oden, it would have committed one of the worst draft-day errors since Portland bypassed Michael Jordan for Sam Bowie. As it transpired, Portland whiffed again in choosing Oden, a potentially great player whose injuries have marred what was a promising career.

A month later, the Celtics chose Georgetown's forward Jeff Green, a talented player but not the keystone arch for a new dynasty. Then the wheels turned, and later that evening a trade between Boston and Seattle was announced: Jeff Green, Wally Szczerbiak, Delonte West, and a future second-rounder for Ray Allen and Glen "Big Baby" Davis. The trade puzzled fans and NBA executives alike. Senior statesman John Havlicek absolutely hated the deal, as did many Boston fans who had seen the Red Sox finally win a World Series but despaired of possibly never seeing another banner raised to the Garden rafters. The Celtics needed defense and youth; instead they got offense and an 11-year NBA vet who played college in Connecticut back when Mark Twain and Harriet Beecher Stowe lived there.

The deal made no sense...unless another shoe was about to drop. On July 31 it finally did, as Ainge and old friend Kevin McHale in Minnesota completed a blockbuster deal: Al Jefferson, Theo Ratliff, Gerald Green, Ryan Gomes, Sebastian Telfair, and two future Celtic first-round draft choices for Kevin Garnett.

One could almost see Red Auerbach in heaven, hell, or Euro-Disney, wherever he was spending his afterlife, lighting up a cigar and saying, "Danny Ainge did that? Danny Ainge? We just got our 17th banner!"

chapter 32
Ubuntu

2007–08

A pleasure from the first tipoff through a long overdue celebration in downtown Boston with duck boats, 2007–08 was the year Banner No. 17 finally came to Boston. Celtics mystique existed, but only with the presence of good ownership, competent management, steady coaching, and All-Star personnel—and now Boston possessed all those elements. Bereft of their usual worrying points, Celtics Nation now had to consume itself with thoughts that super talents like Paul Pierce, Kevin Garnett, and Ray Allen could play nicely together.

Doc Rivers took care of that, preaching the southern African concept of *Ubuntu*, the sacrificing of individual honors for the advancement of group goals. He took some of his players on a duck boat tour of Boston, tracing the route these crazy amphibious vehicles would take them on a parade route if they won a championship. Finally, a trip to Italy to play exhibitions against the Raptors further solidified the group, a hark back to Red Auerbach's odysseys with his men, deep in the Maine woods, uniting his men against any other NBA or semipro club that dared play against them.

Unifying the men did not simply involve getting the Big Three in sync; Danny Ainge needed to add new players to replenish the bench he depleted to obtain Garnett and Allen. He inked two good free agents, guard Eddie House and swingman James Posey. And he had not totally scrapped the youth movement, as Rajon Rondo, Kendrick Perkins, and Tony Allen now had likely matured enough to play with the star veterans.

The Celtics passed their first chemistry test in the Garden in their opener against Washington as Garnett schooled the Wizards with 22 points, 20 rebounds, and five assists, while Pierce and Allen combined for another 45 points. An intense player, Garnett was also one of the most unselfish ones, constantly feeding teammates with scoring opportunities at the expense of his own glory, a trait he transferred to Boston. Ubuntu!

Similarly, ex-Celtics coach (and then Pacers coach) Jim O'Brien shared his observations regarding Paul Pierce: "Paul is a guy that has no problem being an unselfish player. People sometimes misunderstand Paul because the last couple years he had to carry a big load. Paul would have loved people around to shoulder the load."

Unable to defeat the new Celtics conventionally, the Nets tried early in the season to win in a most physically offensive manner, and that backfired too, as a very tough Kevin Garnett observed, "I think it was settled on everyone's mind what kind of game this was going to be, and it was exactly that. It was a come-into-the-bar, I'm-trying-to-find-a-seat, you're-talking-to-my-girl bar fight. Am I lying? That's what it felt like." Garnett got the girl, and the Celtics got the win 91–69.

An early test came at home against Kobe Bryant and the Lakers, and the youth movement won it for Boston. Kendrick Perkins scored 21 and hauled down nine rebounds while point guard Rajon Rondo dished off 10 assists. The veteran Garnett had the last word, though, on this ancient rivalry: "This is my first of, hopefully, many. If you don't know about the Lakers-Celtics history, then you really don't know basketball. I'm looking forward to it and I'm going to enjoy it. I'm going to embrace it."

These Celtics were not single-dimensional basketball drones. Like their multi-talented forebears such as Sam Jones, Bill Sharman, and Chuck Connors, they affected Renaissance Man demeanors. Ray Allen starred as Jesus Shuttlesworth in *He's Got Game*, Pierce played pool, and James Posey bowled. And Rajon Rondo was an accomplished roller skater, working in synchronized pairs or joining with youngsters in a Society for the Prevention of Cruelty skate.

After a win against Toronto on December 16, the Celtics had won 20 of their first 22 games, their finest start since 1963. Three nights later they lost to the Pistons by two points and then thereafter reeled off nine straight victories.

On St. Patrick's Day they started their first leg of the dreaded Texas Triangle, facing San Antonio, Houston, and Dallas in succession. Against the defending champion Spurs, new Celtic Sam Cassell drained a three late for the narrow victory. Ray Allen did not play against the Rockets (Houston then riding a 22-game winning streak), nor did Tony Allen after taking a hard foul and sinking both free throws before leaving the game. No problem; the Celtics held the Rockets to only 74 points as Boston trounced them by 20. Ray Allen came back against the Mavs with a late three-pointer, on a play drawn up for him by Doc Rivers, to complete the Texas sweep.

The biggest duster during the trip may have occurred when Timberwolves owner Glen Taylor accused Garnett of tanking games in his last year in Minnesota, a stupid comment that Kevin dismissed but which Charles Barkley had some fun with: "I like what he said about Glen Taylor; he let that go. That's the difference between me and Kevin Garnett. I can never take the high road." Meanwhile, the smothering Celtics defense answered most other critics as the Celtics won 11 of their last 12 for a 66–16 regular season record.

Then Boston almost threw it all away in the first round of the Eastern Conference playoffs against castoff Joe Johnson and the 37–45 Atlanta Hawks. Ray Allen's scoring touch temporarily deserted him, and Paul Pierce began re-exhibiting some of his past petulance, earning a fine for seemingly flashing the Hawks a gang sign and in another game throwing his headband to the floor. But if Pierce sometimes hurt his team, he also carried his teammates much of the rest of this seven-game series, which culminated in his club's 99–65 blowout victory, punctuated by Pierce's 22 points. Chastened, the Celtics almost treated their recent experience with humility, with Pierce admitting, "We knew we let a couple of games get away in Atlanta. And I just knew we were going to take care of business."

In the semis, LeBron James and the Cavs also took the Celtics to seven before bowing out. Rondo played well, but Ray Allen continued to throw up bricks. The defense, and some key play by reserve P.J. Brown, saved this team again. In the Eastern Conference Finals, the Celtics continued to be haunted by poor personnel moves of the past as they faced Chauncey Billups and the Pistons. Of course, they also faced off against a poor personnel choice of the future, Rasheed Wallace. With James Posey bedeviling Billups on defense, Boston scraped by in six to face the Lakers in the NBA Finals.

Ray Allen had regained his shot, and Paul Pierce, who had toiled for so many awful Boston clubs, had some restored perspective, observing, "It makes me think about a year ago today, what I was doing. To be in this position with the same team going to the Finals, it's nothing I can really put into words."

The Celtics and Lakers frankly did not have much of a rivalry anymore; almost two decades of front office ineptitude on Causeway Street guaranteed that. But this was not the juggernaut Lakers, as L.A. had to rebuild itself after Shaquille O'Neal left, and during this series Paul Pierce defended Kobe Bryant well. Ahead 2–1 going into the fourth game in Los Angeles, it appeared as if the series had tied itself as early as the second quarter when the Lakers led by 24 points. But in the second half, the Celtics' defense held L.A. to just 33 points as they pushed ahead to steal a victory. After a sloppy loss in Game 5, the Celtics came home to bury the Lakers 131–92 at the Garden. After the final buzzer, fans spilled out onto Causeway Street without Lucky or the Celtics dancers or Gino, and like their fathers and mothers once did, danced through the night.

The Boston Celtics were NBA champions again!

2008–09

The title defense essentially ended with Kevin Garnett's right knee injury, diagnosed as a strained tendon sustained in a game against the Jazz on February 19, 2009. He returned briefly but was finished by the end of March, resorting to surgery and the removal of a bone spur. In addition to Garnett, Tony Allen broke his thumb, Brian Scalabrine sustained multiple concussions, Rajon Rondo and Glen Davis each sprained an ankle.

The reigning champions defended their title without the services of James Posey, who left for New Orleans via free agency, and P.J. Brown and Sam Cassell had played their last games in the NBA. But it was the injuries that killed this team, because early in the season, the Celtics excelled, reeling off a 19-game winning streak and then later, a 12-game streak. Remarkably, even with these injuries, Doc coached this club to 62 victories.

In the playoffs, though, they barely squeaked by their first-round opponent, Derrick Rose's Bulls, and lost another key player, Leon Powe, in the second game, sidelined by a torn left ACL, although he played with the injury for three minutes after sustaining it. Tony Allen received death threats in Chicago while Bulls management spread rose petals around the court to honor Derrick Rose's selection as Rookie of the Year. This was the series of overtimes; in fact, it was the longest series in NBA history, with two single-overtimes, a double OT, and a triple OT, games that taxed an already depleted roster. At the end, an exultant Paul Pierce conceded, "We really didn't expect them to play the way they did through the whole seven games. We expected them to play hard, but they really pushed us to the limit. It was a great, great series. Thank goodness we were battle-tested and we had experience in seventh games."

Fatigued and playing without Garnett or Powe, the Celtics bowed to Dwight Howard's Magic in seven in the next round. Rashard Lewis killed them, particularly in the last game with threes swishing all over the place. Orlando made 13 of 21 threes while Boston converted on only 4-of-16, a point not lost on Doc Rivers: "Every shot was front rim, every free throw was off, we were slow to get to the basket.... We just didn't have it."

Glen Davis filled in well, particularly in some of the playoff games, but the hoped-for spark in signing Stephon Marbury did not materialize. Like past great Celtics teams, it was time to tweak the roster.

The next year held promise with a healthy Garnett, a point made by Brian Scalabrine in his own transition from a player to a commentator: "I know one thing: we're definitely going to be geared up to win a championship, no matter who's on the team. We're not going to be playing just to make it; we're going to playing to win a championship. We're a championship team, we have a window of opportunity, and we need to take advantage of that."

2009–10

Doc Rivers guided the Celtics to the seventh game of the NBA Finals in 2009–10, quite a feat with a team that won only 50 games in the regular season. It did not start out in such a forlorn fashion; for instance, on Christmas Day, without Paul Pierce, Boston defeated the Orlando Magic of Dwight Howard, Rashard Lewis, and Vince Carter. The Celtics had compiled a 23–5 record and then went 27–27 the rest of the season. Too often the Big Three of Pierce, Garnett, and Ray Allen did not play together.

Veteran additions in the guise of Michael Finley and Rasheed Wallace did not work, with Wallace the biggest disappointment, though a February trade brought in Nate Robinson, who performed well and often joyously. Instead of tough defensive presence down low, Wallace was a guy who turned it over all the time and insisted on taking threes all night, despite posting one of the historically worst seasons doing so in NBA history.

Unlike the previous year, the Celtics had put their injuries behind them, and a healthy team overran the Heat in the first round of the playoffs, with Rajon Rondo demonstrating increasing poise in important games. Similarly, against the Cavaliers in the semis, they rolled, with LeBron James at times appearing as though he simply had given up. In Game 6 of the conference finals, Allen scored 20 points, and Nate Robinson—with 13 points in the second quarter alone—buried the Magic as Boston jetted to L.A. for an appointment with the Lakers.

Ahead 3–2 heading to L.A., Boston not only lost the sixth game but its center Kendrick Perkins with PCL and MCL tears, causing Pierce to lament, "We need his size and his rebounding and his defense. Perk is our enforcer, a guy who pushes guys with his body and his length, gets guys off rebounds."

Even without Perkins, the Celtics nearly won Game 7 and the title, leading in L.A. after three quarters, as Wallace played well as the new center. Unfortunately, the Lakers went on a run in the fourth, ending the season unsatisfactorily for the Celtics and their Nation.

In sunny Los Angeles, Rajon Rondo warned, "We're in for a long summer."

2010–11

During the off-season, the Miami Heat had assembled its own Big Three: LeBron James, Dwyane Wade, and Chris Bosh. No matter, at least at the outset; Boston defeated this supergroup on opening night and pretty much kept winning until Christmas, kicking off the holidays at 23–4.

Not since Bill Russell had stepped down had there been such a rush on centers in Boston, this despite Kendrick Perkins entering his eighth season in the pivot. Hoping to squeeze one more year out of Shaquille O'Neal and Jermaine O'Neal, Danny Ainge signed them both. Previously, he had drafted Turkish seven-footer Semih Erden and later signed up Chris Johnson to a 10-day contract, so it appeared as if the Celtics at least contemplated their options with Perkins about to fulfill the last year of his contract, rehabbing from surgery due to a torn anterior cruciate ligament.

As expected, the Celtics started their season with Shaq at center, surrounded by Kevin Garnett, Paul Pierce, Ray Allen, and Rajon Rondo. Doc used his bench liberally, but as feared, injuries overtook this team, with Jermaine O'Neal falling in November with a left knee injury, Delonte West with a broken right wrist, and Rajon Rondo with a strained left hammy. By Thanksgiving, this team lacked much to be thankful for. Nate Robinson filled in well for Rondo, but then Shaq joined the other O'Neal with his own knee injury.

Everyone seemed to squeeze into this roster: Luke Harangody, Sasha Pavlovic, Carlos Arroyo, Chris Johnson, Von Wafer, Troy Murphy, Helen of Troy, the man on the Quaker Oats box, and the ghost of Ed Sadowski. Sick of injuries, Rondo dislocated his shoulder one night, popped it back in, and returned to action.

The whole scheme depended on a healthy Shaq in the playoffs, and as soon as it fell apart, it spurred a bad decision, namely by triggering one of the team's most controversial transactions, swapping Kendrick Perkins and Nate Robinson to the Thunder for center Nenad Krstic, forward Jeff Green, and a first-round pick that turned out to be Fab Melo. The Celtics needed a center, and they lost the youngest and healthiest one they had.

Bringing in Troy Murphy as a free agent backfired also, and although the Celts swept the Knicks in the first round of the playoffs this year, the Heat ended it all for Boston in five in the Eastern Conference semis.

Doc Rivers' contract was up. Suddenly these Boston Celtics looked old.

2011–12

The lockout year started on Christmas Day, 2011, and improbably ended after the seventh game of the Eastern Conference Finals against the Miami Heat, as the Celtics nearly dethroned the dynastic apparents.

Doc Rivers had the opportunity of walking out on Boston and preserving a legacy or hanging in with his players in sickness and in health; Doc signed up again as the coach to the relief of Danny Ainge and his players.

Heart defined this team of aging veterans, personified by the fierce Kevin Garnett, proving that rumors of his demise were premature. There are so many good things to say about Garnett as a player; the only negative for Celtics fans is that he did not play his whole career here. Red Auerbach once said that Bailey Howell was always a Celtic, it just took him awhile to get there. The same can be said for Garnett.

Like Bill Russell, Garnett played with intensity yet was an extraordinarily unselfish teammate. Garnett led the NBA in total points on only one occasion (2003–04, his MVP season) but easily could have led in that category on other occasions had he not deferred to teammates so often and at his own statistical expense. On the offensive end, at age 35, he still tallied 15.8 points per game.

Maladies threatened to derail this team early, as Jeff Green received a diagnosis of aortic aneurysm, requiring open-heart surgery that disabled him for the campaign. After losing to Oklahoma City on February 22, Boston's fifth consecutive defeat, this very old-looking team stood at 15–17.

To their credit, the Celtics refused to script their own obituary. A December pickup worked very well for them, as they obtained Brandon Bass from the Magic in exchange for Glen Davis and Von Wafer. This one slipped by most fans, as the radio shows churned a constant refrain to deal off Rajon Rondo. Suspended for two games for throwing a ball at an official, Rondo soon replaced petulance with triple-doubles, helping to kick-start the team to some modest winning streaks as he and his veteran Big Three teammates led Boston to an Atlantic Division title.

The region's fandom embraced this team, particularly when juxtaposed with the underperforming Red Sox, a baseball club characterized by discord, laziness, unprofessionalism, and undeserved privilege topped off with generous helpings of chicken wings and beer. There were no Ws or Ls on the Red Sox's paychecks.

In the 1980s, most people knew better than to upset Larry Bird, and Atlanta Hawks owner Michael Gearon risked a backlash by referring to Kevin Garnett as the "dirtiest player in the league" in the opening round of the NBA playoffs. Garnett repaid the compliment by leading the Celts past Atlanta in the sixth and deciding game of the series with 28 points and 14 rebounds, driving to the basket with extreme prejudice.

Seemingly the luck of the Celtics held out with the draw of the eighth seed in the Eastern Conference semis, but the young Sixers took it to seven before succumbing. In another classic seventh game at the Garden, Paul Pierce fouled out with 4:16 left in the game, but Rajon Rondo scored almost half of his points, on the way to a triple-double, from that point on to nail the win and the right to play Miami in the Eastern Conference Finals.

The hated Heat, swagger personified. Yet heading into the fourth quarter of Game 7, the score at American Airlines Arena stood tied at 73–73. Despite the absence of a post presence and a squad that featured more jumpers than the girls department at J.C. Penney's in the 1960s, this veteran club had stalemated a constellation of opposing supernovas.

Unfortunately, in that last period, Dwyane Wade ended his hibernation, Chris Bosh played well, and LeBron buried Boston. There would not be another legendary seventh-game victory for the Celtics, at least not on this night.

Still, it was a team of champions.

2012–13

The breakup of Boston's Big Three came from within, as Ray Allen reportedly turned down more money from the Celtics to sign as a free agent with Miami and form the Heat's Big Four.

The remaining Celtics soldiered on, fighting off Father Time—rumor had it that the 2012–13 season could be Kevin Garnett's last—and injury. Rajon Rondo missed more than half of the campaign after tearing an ACL, and soon thereafter promising forward Jared Sullinger went on injured reserve. Increasingly, younger players such as Avery Bradley and Jeff Green began taking on more responsibilities.

The Celtics never did play their final home game of the season; driven by security fears after the terrorist attacks at the Boston Marathon, the game was canceled and the team closed out an unsatisfying 41–40.

In the first round of the playoffs, the Celtics met their rivals from New York, a Knicks team led by the perimeter-oriented attack of Carmelo Anthony and Sixth Man of the Year J.R. Smith. Facing elimination in Game 6 at the Garden, the Celtics found themselves down by as many as 26 points in the fourth quarter, but, true to their leaders' nature, the team fought back and sliced the lead to four before its season finally ended.

Alas, all good things must end, and the Ubuntu-era Celtics did in a decisive and calculated manner. After a flurry of rumors and non-denials, Doc Rivers was released from the remaining years on his Celtics contract and high-tailed it to Los Angeles to take over the suddenly formidable Clippers. (Boston received a first-round pick in 2015 from L.A. in return.) Shortly thereafter, the club shipped Jason Terry, Garnett, and Pierce to the Brooklyn Nets for a package of players, picks, flotsam, and jetsam. The trading of Pierce, in particular, was hard to stomach for Boston fans, who had long hoped the forward would retire a Celtic, but Ainge stayed true to his belief that it's better to say good-bye too soon than too late. To complete the upheaval, the club hired Brad Stevens, the bright young coach who had led Butler University to two national championship games, and gave him a six-year contract.

The Celtics are changing again, but two irreducible facts remain: there is still plenty of room left on the rafters for championship banners, and that someday, the Celtics will fill them.

Acknowledgments

I would like to profusely thank the staffs at the Professional Basketball Hall of Fame and the Sports Museum. Richard Johnson at the Sports Museum was a huge help when I encountered detours in the road. Brockton's Jack McCormick set screens and helped in transition. Phil Bissell provided some very useful historical information, and as Phil would put it, occasionally hysterical information. The players of the past whom I spoke to were all generous with their time, not to mention friendly and professional. Thanks to Lori Hubbard and Billy Hubbard for editing assistance.

I relied on Basketball-Reference.com for much of my statistical research and deliberately used the term NBA to refer to every league that the Celtics were involved in.

Much love to Lori, Billy, and Caroline Hubbard.